THE BIRTH AND IMPACT OF BRITPOP

THE BIRTH AND IMPACT OF BRITPOP

MIS-SHAPES, SCENESTERS AND INSATIABLE ONES

PAUL LAIRD

WHITE OWL
AN IMPRINT OF PEN & SWORD BOOKS LTD.
YORKSHIRE – PHILADELPHIA

First published in Great Britain in 2022 by
PEN AND SWORD WHITE OWL
An imprint of
Pen & Sword Books Ltd
Yorkshire - Philadelphia

ISBN 978 1 39901 747 3

Typeset in Times New Roman 12/16 by SJmagic DESIGN SERVICES, India.
Printed and bound in the UK by CPI Group (UK) Ltd.

Pen & Sword Books Ltd incorporates the Imprints of Pen & Sword Books
Archaeology, Atlas, Aviation, Battleground, Discovery, Family History,
History, Maritime, Military, Naval, Politics, Railways, Select, Transport, True
Crime, Fiction, Frontline Books, Leo Cooper, Praetorian Press, Seaforth
Publishing, Wharncliffe and White Owl.

For a complete list of Pen & Sword titles please contact
PEN & SWORD BOOKS LIMITED
47 Church Street, Barnsley, South Yorkshire, S70 2AS, England
E-mail: enquiries@pen-and-sword.co.uk
Website: www.pen-and-sword.co.uk

Or
PEN AND SWORD BOOKS
1950 Lawrence Rd, Havertown, PA 19083, USA
E-mail: Uspen-and-sword@casematepublishers.com
Website: www.penandswordbooks.com

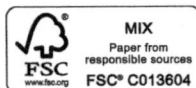

MIX
Paper from
responsible sources
FSC
www.fsc.org   FSC® C013604

Contents

Author's Note

This is not *the* story of Britpop. Maybe *the* story of Britpop doesn't actually exist. There are books that carefully and precisely document the socio-political aspects of Britpop, there are books that provide oral histories of the period, there are novels with Britpop as a setting and there are encyclopedias of Britpop. This book isn't any of those things.

This is a story of Britpop, but it is *my* story. This is the story of a most extraordinary moment in British popular culture as experienced by a most ordinary boy. I have a suspicion that my story is not unique and that over the course of this book you might recognise yourself.

I have tried to write about the bands and the artists that captured the spirit of the time...even if lots of people haven't ever heard of them. Britpop wasn't ever about rock 'n' roll, bucket hats and lads for kids like me, it was the moment when indie music and the indie aesthetic burst into the mainstream. From 1991-1994 the mis-shapes became, whisper it, cool. It didn't last, how could it, but it set the tone for the cultural revolution that followed. If this book is anything, it is a love letter to the people and the music that mattered to me and the kids who were just like me...and you?

Prologue

When Margaret Thatcher left Downing Street, in November of 1990, most people believed that not only was it the end of *her* time in office, but that it was the end for a deeply unpopular Government. The Conservative Party that she had led since 1975 was fractured, and for many voters, across the UK, particularly the young, they were seen as something much worse than 'the nasty party'. The destruction of mining communities, Section 28, the privatisation of previously publicly owned services, record unemployment, a war over the Falklands and much more had all combined to make them a toxic brand. Many of us believed that the General Election of 1992 would usher in a Labour government and put Neil Kinnock inside number ten. Things, of course, didn't quite work out that way with the grey man of politics, John Major, leading the Conservatives to a fourth term in office. The fact that Labour hadn't been able to land the knock-out blow when they were on the ropes was a cause for much wailing and gnashing of teeth on the left. Parallels with Corbynism's failure to prevent a Boris Johnson premiership, and the omnishambles that has followed, are difficult to ignore.

Major presented a romantic vision of Britain's past in October 1993 when he gave a speech outlining what he saw as core British values such as being neighbourly, decency, good manners, respect for the law, personal responsibility and family values. On the surface there was little to disagree with in this view of Britain and Britishness, even if the truth of the country's past was less idyllic, and few could find any real reason to oppose these principles as the bedrock for a successful and harmonious nation. The truth of what this 'back to basics' vision meant though was soon laid bare, when Conservative MPs like John Redwood and Peter Lilley launched blistering attacks on teenage mothers and an ugly tone of moral superiority took root on a variety of other social and sexual issues. The fact that Major himself was involved in an extra-marital affair at the time with another Tory MP (Edwina Currie) and that a veritable smorgasbord of other sexual shenanigans were being engaged in by a number of other high profile Tories meant that they were, once again, on the ropes and ripe for a battering at the polls.

1992 had seen the 'grunge invasion', spearheaded by Nirvana, with lots of boys and girls from America finding themselves with record contracts, chart successes and prime spots on bedroom walls, despite the fact that they had none of the more recognisable qualities of pop stars, primarily tunes or melodies. That they were also dressed in the sort of wardrobe that would make even the most sartorially challenged think twice simply added insult to injury for those of us who believed that pop stars should sparkle. Of course grunge wasn't really about pop, it was rock music - without any of the roll. It presented a bleak, nihilistic and hopeless vision to its audience and in bleak, nihilistic and hopeless times it seemed perfect.

That inability of Neil Kinnock and the Labour Party to oust the Tories in the General Election of April 1992 served to plunge young people like me into a state of near terminal malady. Kenneth Williams' last diary entry, written four years earlier, summed up our mood: 'Oh, what's the bloody point?'. Even as we watched one Tory politician after another get caught shagging someone who wasn't their wife, sometimes while wearing a football[1] shirt,

---

1. Conservative politician, David Mellor was accused by his mistress, Antonia de Sancha of having enjoyed intimate moments while wearing a replica football shirt-in 2013 she admitted that she had made the story up.

despite having appeared on television just hours before droning on about 'family values' we just knew that they were going to win next time too. Unemployment was on the rise again with some 3 million people out of work. The economy was beginning to exit a recession but times were tough for many, particularly the young. This was what Britain was. A hopeless island led by hypocrites. This was the fertile soil in which grunge could plant itself, take root and grow.

They were rotten days.

The thrills of Madchester with ecstasy, Joe Bloggs jeans and the blissed out grooves and melodies of The Stone Roses, seemed like a very long time ago. That second summer of love mingled with the first rush of ecstasy had been extinguished by the press who could barely conceal their delight at the tragic death of Leah Betts, a policeman's daughter who died after dropping a tab. The press, erroneously, reported that this was the first time that she had taken the drug, in fact she had done so on three previous occasions. Her death was exactly what the Government needed to stamp out the rave scene of the early nineties. Drugs, we had learned from Zammo and the Grange Hill gang, were bad - always and in all circumstances. That included MDMA, and the war on drugs turned to the rave scene, raised a boot and stamped down hard.

The notion of some sort of fightback against the lank hair and lumpen anti-melodies of grunge as well as against the brutal Conservative government began, for many casual observers, with the release of 'Popscene' by Blur in March 1992. A furious, fierce, ferocious and frenzied blast of pop, punk, pop-punk, punk-pop and attitude that should have seen Blur hailed as the future of British music. Instead it failed to break into the top thirty, was slammed by the music press and left the band on the brink of, well, not being a band. It was, however, the blueprint for what was to come. For Blur the failure of the single could have signalled the end, the fact that it didn't says much about their drive and determination as well as the loyalty of their label.

But this is a lazy version of the Britpop story. The truth is that the template had been crafted in 1991 and 1992 by two bands and two albums, each of which had one foot in the past, one in the present and both eyes fixed firmly on the future. First came Saint Etienne's 'Fox Base Alpha' in 1991, a record that blended baggy beats, dance, a cultured Europhile sensibility and a uniquely Anglophile take on everything. It's retro from the get-go with imagery, modernist stylings and an icy cool attitude that set it very far apart from almost everything else going on in British pop at the time. Then came the greatest glam rock album not made by a glam rock band: 'Back in Denim' by Denim. The brainchild of former Felt frontman Lawrence (no surname required) this was the album that most clearly predicted where British music would turn next for inspiration, with everyone from the sexually ambiguous likes of Suede to the lads of Oasis drawing inspiration from the same acts that Lawrence was channeling here: Bowie, Slade, T-Rex and the rest. Together these are the two albums that paved the way for Britpop.

What these albums also reveal is that despite the awfulness of Britain at the start of the nineties there were still creative and inspirational faces trying to craft works of wonder as an escape from, or reflection of, the misery around them. That 'Back in Denim' sounds, and looks, like it could have been released during the winter of discontent is no accident as Lawrence was drawing clear parallels between the state of the nation in 1978 and 1991 - soaring unemployment, economic recession, unpopular government. It was an arch and knowing piece of pop art and the fact that it remains largely unremarked on by other commentators on the era is terribly sad.

Britpop didn't exist at this point. It was a whisper. A nameless, shapeless form lurking in the cupboard under pop music's stairs.

A pop Babadook[2]. It would take the frenzy that surrounded the arrival of Suede following the release of their debut single 'The Drowners', a few weeks after 'Popscene', on 11 May 1992 for that whisper to grow to a murmur and morph from a shadowy figure to a technicolour presence.

Then in April 1993, Select magazine ran a cover story that boldly proclaimed 'Yanks Go Home', with Brett Anderson superimposed on top of a Union Flag. It was a provocative, arguably xenophobic, move on the part of the magazine and one that would coin the term 'Britpop' as well as stir the pot of patriotism and nationalism.

A few years earlier the NME had covered Morrissey's appearance at the Madstock[3] festival in London's Finsbury Park, where the Pope of Mope had sashayed across the stage in front of a crowd made up of a small pocket of his most dedicated followers as well as many who were less enamoured by his presence. The majority of the audience were there for Madness and, through no fault of their own, that has often included members of the far right. Draping himself in a Union Flag and with a Derek Ridgers photo of two skinhead girls as his backdrop, Morrissey was playing with fire. This, for the NME, was enough to suggest that Mozzer was 'flirting with disaster[4]'. It led to a bitter divorce between the star and the paper as well as to a forensic examination of his views on race that didn't cast him in a particularly positive light.

---

2. Jennifer Kent's 2014 psychological horror film is built around the notion that the traumas of her past have taken physical form in the basement of her home. While initially threatening to destroy her she learns to tame the monster and live peacefully alongside it. Sadly, Britpop couldn't manage the same trick with Oasis.
3. A two day festival curated by Madness
4. NME, 22 August 1992 ran with the headline 'Morrissey Flying the Flag or Flirting with Disaster?'

Now just three years later the flag was being reclaimed and Britishness was being recast as something to be proud of, a fierce last stand against American cultural imperialism. Or something.

Select had gathered together the bands whom they felt best captured the cultural mood of the nation: Suede, Saint Etienne, Denim, The Auteurs and Pulp. Despite the enormous success that would follow for some of those bands and for the myriad others who would come later, the truth is that this is the best representation of what Britpop was - fringe figures, eccentrics, pop music obsessives, arch, knowing and peculiar people with stars in their eyes and glitter in their souls. Happier with David Essex in 'Stardust' than they were with Sting in 'Quadrophenia'.

Each of the bands, aside from Suede, were asked the same questions to gauge how closely aligned they were and, I would guess, to try and stoke up some sort of us against them battle of the bands/nations with the grunge gang. Despite what The Guardian has had to say on Britpop in articles with titles like 'Don't Look Back in Anger: did Britpop Cause Brexit?'[5] the responses to some of those questions reveal much less support for a Rule Britannia mindset or a Little Englander worldview than one might have imagined.

When asked to reveal what they thought was so great about Britain and British pop, Bob Stanley of Saint Etienne said that he preferred France, Jarvis Cocker talked about the sense of romance and Luke Haines of The Auteurs bluntly revealed that he didn't think there was anything great about either Britain or its pop music. Just as revealing were the responses to a question about what made them ashamed to be British. Bob Stanley talked passionately about our dreadful record on accepting refugees from what was then Yugoslavia, Sarah Cracknell blasted the royal

---

5. Michael Hann, The Guardian, November 2018

family, Jarvis took a shot at football casuals (ironic given what was to come later in the Britpop story) and then Luke Haines had this to say: 'Plenty of things. The racism. All that despicable British Movement crap'.

I think it is safe to say that none of these people believed that they were participating in laying the groundwork for a renaissance in British nationalism. Here, explicitly, key movers and shakers in this new moment in British pop music were talking about romantic notions of Britishness, the ridiculousness of the British class system, the vulgarity of some aspects of British culture and denouncing, quite clearly, racism in any form. Of course none of this means that jingoism, maybe nationalism, didn't rear its head during the nineties but what it does show is that none of the bands were directly promoting any such agenda. How individuals choose to interpret art isn't really the responsibility of the artist and if anyone is to blame for the more laddish and overtly nationalistic tone of some moments of the era it is the press and not the artists.

There is something quite depressing too in the fact that here we are nearly thirty years later and the very things that were problematic for the people in those bands about Britain then remain problematic today; the country's response to refugee crises, the rise of expressly nationalistic political movements, racism, hooliganism, the Monarchy. Same as it ever was, same as it ever was.

I can't be critical of Select and the journalists who drove this issue as I bought into the 'British Image #1'[6] thing hook, line and sinker. The Britpop scene was a tidal wave of joy for me at the time and the music continues to bring warm feelings and good memories years later. I think the intentions of Andrew Harrison,

---

6. At the time of the release of Blur's 'Modern Life is Rubbish' album there were photographs of the band in front of this slogan spray painted on a wall.

a fine writer and good person, were entirely honourable when he wrote this:

> 'Yet at its best the Union Jack used to represent all that Suede, Denim, Saint Etienne and the other bands in this issue embody: tolerance, pride without hatred, humour, openness, tenacity, decency, optimism, invention and, above all, community spirit…'

This was a rallying call to those of a liberal disposition to reclaim the flag from those who had drenched it in racism, fascism and intolerance and repurpose it as something more inclusive. That was always going to be tough but, for a while at least, it did seem as though the country as a whole was finding a way to do just that. Ginger Spice in her Union Jack dress, Noel Gallagher with his Union Jack guitar and Sonya Madan[7] with her 'My Home Too' Union Jack t-shirt all displayed a version of the flag that was different to that associated with football hooligans having a tear up in some European country or other. New Labour played a part in this too, utilising the flag as a means to show floating voters, as well as Wet Tories, that they were patriots too and not evil old Trots like Michael Foot. It worked and helped to deliver a landslide victory in 1997. It all seemed to be going well.

It couldn't last.

The Union Jack brand had been too sullied for too long. History shows that Luke Haines was right to be suspicious at the start - not because the label Britpop was inherently toxic and certainly not because it paved the way for what has happened in the last few years in British politics but because the use of the flag has allowed certain types of people to claim that anyone who walks beneath it approves of everything done when it flies. The

---

7. Lead singer with Echobelly

real heart of Britpop doesn't lie in the Union Jack backdrop but in the responses given above by key figures in the era.

Britpop was fun, throwaway, energetic, occasionally magnificent, sometimes awful, creative, spiky, retro and forward looking, often all at the same time. It wasn't ever about being 'British' either - not for me, not for those of us who were there before the arrival of Loaded and lad culture. It wasn't about your passport or your place of birth. It wasn't about identity but about identifying. It was a moment when outsiders, no matter where they came from, found themselves at the centre of everything. It was about youth. It was about hope. It helped to foster the energy required to oust a loathed government and usher in something we all hoped would be better.

There are legitimate criticisms to be made of the scene: the vulgar sexism of lad culture, the absence of BAME voices and faces, and the narrow range of influences. But, crucially, many of those criticisms apply to what followed on from the arrival of Oasis and do not apply to the art school fops who announced the arrival of what would be labelled Britpop. Denim had nothing in common with Oasis, Saint Etienne were not Cast, The Auteurs don't occupy the same space as Ocean Colour Scene.

This book is an attempt to focus on the bands who thrilled young people like me during the nineties. We were the boys and girls who would have been bullied in the playground by the lads who would later be found prowling the crowds of Oasis concerts, clad in terrace clobber and howling with laughter at eccentrics like The Vessel from David Devant and His Spirit Wife and nodding in agreement when Noel Gallagher wished death from AIDS on members of Blur. This was the real battle of Britpop and, in many corners of social media, it is still being waged.

Chapter 1

Madchester, So Much To Answer For

The scene before the scene.

In December of 1943 in the city of Evansville, Indiana, the Washington family welcomed a baby boy whom they named William Francis. By the time William Washington was twenty two he was stationed in England with the United States Air Force. Going by the name 'Geno', he was a well-known face on the live music scene in London, regularly standing in as a vocalist for groups. One evening in a nightclub, guitarist Pete Gage saw Geno performing and asked him to join his new band, which would become Geno Washington and the Ram Jam Band and have two of the biggest selling albums of the sixties: 'Hand Clappin', Foot Stompin', Funky-Butt…Live' and 'Hipster Flipster Finger Poppin' Daddies'.

This handsome young African American soul singer would become the inspiration for the number one single 'Geno' by Dexys Midnight Runners in March of 1980 and, more importantly for our story, he may also be the man responsible for Britpop.

Following a gig in Manchester in 1983, [1] Washington was invited to a gathering somewhere in the city. Never a man to turn his back on such an invite he accepted and found himself in the company of a gaggle of young Manchester faces. As the evening progressed he found himself drawn towards a young man who was

---

1. This is the story as told in John Robb's book 'The Stone Roses and the Resurrection of British Pop'

1

the object of obvious desire from most of the girls in the room as well as being the centre of attention for most of the boys. That this young man helped him secure some 'blow' simply cemented Geno's interest in him. 'Do you sing?' he asked the boy, 'Nah' was the reply but he did write poetry. 'If you can write poetry then you can write lyrics, that's where the money is in the music business. You should be in a band, man, you're good looking, people love you. You should be in a band.'

Two years later that kid, Ian Brown, released a single, 'So Young' with his band The Stone Roses and the stage was set for a revolution in British music the likes of which hadn't been seen, or heard, since the arrival of the Sex Pistols.

At around the same time that The Stone Roses dropped 'So Young' another gaggle of Mancunian boys released their first records. The Happy Mondays, signed to the iconic Factory label, hit turntables in 1985 with '45' and then 'Freaky Dancing' a year later. While the Mondays had been together, in some form or another, since 1980 it wasn't until the arrival of the Roses that a 'scene', albeit nascent, began to emerge. There would be no overnight success for either band but within three years the cult following they had built in Manchester had transformed into nationwide recognition and adoration.

In an early television interview[2] with Brown and the man who would craft the melodies that would define the sound of guitar music for the next twenty years, John Squire, they were asked what the best thing that anyone had said about their band had been. After a deafening silence Brown managed to grunt that he didn't know before Squires said that, if they were being honest, they weren't all that interested in the band.

For two young men who hadn't yet become one of the most lauded bands in British music history this was, even by Manchester

---

2. Music Box, 1989

standards, a level of arrogance rarely seen before. Of course it may not have been arrogance, they may have meant it. Maybe what really mattered to the Roses wasn't the band but the music?

Their eponymous debut album was released in the spring of 1989 and that same week I found myself being summoned to the home of Dave, my friend and musical guru. When I arrived I was barely able to say 'Hello' to his mum before Dave was dragging me to his bedroom. 'Listen to THIS…' he said before he pushed play on the tape deck. In anticipation of my arrival he had already cued it up to play the third track, 'Waterfall'.

When it finished he stopped the tape and then turned to look at me, grinning. I didn't know what to say. He just kept looking at me, urging me to give him the correct answer without saying anything. Waiting. Anticipating. 'Play it again?' I said. That was exactly what he had been waiting for. Clearly he had been doing this over and over before I arrived because he hit rewind and then play at exactly the right spot. Later he confessed this was exactly what he had been doing.

Play. Stop. Rewind. Stop. Play.

I hadn't really heard it the first time he played it. I had felt it. Become lost in it. Something beautiful washed over me. Like the first warm day after winter. It unlocked a part of me that I didn't know existed. Now, as we listened a second time, I felt all of that again and heard hope and possibility - my dreams were brought closer with every shimmering guitar hook and every delicate brush of the drums, the swell of the bass line and the innocence of the voice.

Dave and I listened to the whole album that night. Twice. The first time for me to listen and the second time so that Dave could make me a copy on a blank tape. I always took a blank tape to Dave's house. His bedroom was like a library of new music. Every time I went he played something by someone I didn't know. His walls were decorated with posters and postcards of bands I had

3

never heard of, copies of the NME littered the floor. He wasn't the cool kid at school - except he actually *was* the cool kid at school, it was just that none of us had noticed.

People often see that album, maybe even the Roses themselves, as some sort of sixties revivalists. Later in the same Music Box interview where they had declared themselves to be utterly uninterested in the band, they were asked what was the most hurtful thing anyone had ever said about them. This time there was no hesitation as Brown replied, 'That we're influenced by the sixties. Keeps me awake at night.'

'The Stone Roses' isn't a sixties album. It's difficult to see how anyone ever really thought it was. Lazy thinking. Easy touchstones. It's a psychedelic, hazy, lazy Sunday afternoon of an album in places. A strident, powerful but delicate and beautiful album. It's not Herman's Hermits or the Droning Bones though. What it really is, is the sound of the now, informed by the past, maybe, but it's also the sound of the future. A rejection of nostalgia, a manifesto for a new generation.

It really was an album that changed everything, at least for a while. I know, you've heard that before. Usually from blokes with dreadful haircuts who have squeezed their beer guts into a Penguin polo shirt for a night out without their wife. Droning on about the Roses while you try to get a drink at the bar. Fading casuals with a photograph of Paul Weller in their wallets for when they go to the barber[3]. But they are right about this album.

From the cover with its nod to the 1968 student riots in France and some Jackson Pollock vibes to the loops and swoops of the music, instantly recognisable and yet completely alien all at once. The imperfect vocals from Ian Brown. The haircuts. The flares.

---

3. These men are often known as 'Wellends' and a Google image search for that term will see you transported into a world of unimaginable horrors.

The swagger. It all just seemed *perfect*. Something was happening in British music.

At the same time as the delicate delights of the Roses, with their modernist take on past delights in pop 'n' roll history, there were the scallies of the Happy Mondays. Led by Shaun William Ryder they were something altogether more dangerous, more peculiar and more terrifying than any of their contemporaries. Often bands make great play of their working class credentials, or the pain of their childhoods when, in fact, they are grammar school boys whose idea of trauma is not being able to go on the sixth form ski trip to Courchevel. However, with the Mondays we were, very definitely, dealing with genuine working class anti-heroes.

Ryder was the son of a postman (Derek, who would later be the band's tour manager) and a nurse, Linda. Growing up in Little Hulton made him a Salfordian - the same area of Manchester that had been home to little Steven Morrissey some years earlier. Famously, Morrissey had opined that there might be a little bit more to life than reading while never actually giving any indication that he had experienced anything other than words on the page. Ryder, however, left school at thirteen and started working on a building site. Libraries may well be a source of power and inspiration but for Shaun, it would be the university of life that fired his creativity.

Famously, Factory Records supremo Tony Wilson compared Ryder's writing to that of W.B Yeats. He never backed down on this assertion, always insisting that Ryder was a poet and like all great poets he drew on his own life for inspiration. His songs were full of energy, adventure, drugs and sex - just like the Mondays themselves.

They were a band who lived every moment. There were no limits to their ambitions or their appetites. You cannot help but think that the focus on the latter came at the detriment of the former. They could have been the biggest band in the world - but after less than a handful of albums and a clutch of hit singles they were all over bar the shouting.

For different reasons the Stone Roses also failed to become the band they could have been. They were an inspiration to every British guitar band who followed and yet they never quite reached the heights of those that followed them. Record label disputes, personal issues, creative differences all combined to provide just one more album, five years after the debut, and a farewell that was whispered.

Where the Roses and Mondays faded, or imploded, there were other bands in the Madchester scene who not only forged lengthy, and wildly successful, careers but who were at the very heart of what unfolded during the Britpop era - and who have lasted long after that scene died too.

Perhaps the band who emerged as part of Madchester who have had the most significant impact on Britpop and who released some of the most memorable singles of that era are The Charlatans. It would be silly to argue about who was better between the Roses, the Mondays and the Charlies - the answer is always The Charlatans.

Let's look at the numbers first: thirteen albums stretching from their debut 'Some Friendly' in 1990 to, arguably, the peak of their career in 2017 with 'Different Daze'. Then there are over forty singles, twenty-two of which went top forty in the UK and four of them breaking the top ten. This is more than the Roses and the Mondays managed to cobble together between them.

Tim Burgess, The Charlatans' front man, isn't just a songwriter - he is also a lyricist and an author. During the lockdown of 2020 (and on) he has also turned some of his attention to hosting online listening parties - he is the baggy renaissance man, a pop star Lorenzo De' Medici.

The Charlatans have developed the sound of the band with each album, while always remaining identifiably themselves. They are a rock and roll band. They are a pop group. They write music that makes you dance, that lifts your spirits and that helps get you out of bed.

The Charlatans have lost two band members, Jon Brookes and Rob Collins, both of whom have passed away, since their debut and in the face of the loss of two colleagues, two friends, two loved ones, the band has shown incredible heart and soul. Mourning and grieving with dignity, acknowledging the beauty of the people they lost and then, in the best possible way, marking the passing of kindred spirits by carrying on and doing the very things that had bound them together in the first place. Moving on but never moving away.

A lot of bands release a great debut album and follow it up with a solid second and from then on it can be the law of diminishing returns - records that sound a bit like the band you fell in love with but without any of the heart that took you there. They may even contain individual tracks that are loaded with the genius of their best work but it's never quite as good. Not so with The Charlatans. This is a band who can, legitimately, lay claim to their latest work being their best work, and that's quite the claim when you consider that before Different Days' their previous album 'Modern Nature' had also staked a claim to be their career best, which isn't bad going given that their debut album was released nearly thirty years ago.

Back in 1990, I was seventeen and so far from being cool that I was possibly too cool, whatever the hell that means. I had arrived late to The Smiths party and was sporting a quiff, a blouse from Evans and a pair of baggy, but not 'baggy', Levi's. My party piece at the local indie disco[4] was to whip off my shirt and flail

---

4. Bentleys in Kirkcaldy held a student night every Thursday. It usually attracted a 'crowd' of about a dozen people.

around the dance floor whenever 'This Charming Man'[5] was played (which it was every week because I brought it with me) before spending the remainder of the night sat in a corner reading 'Catcher in the Rye' (form an orderly queue ladies) and then heading home to cry myself to sleep. That meant that I missed the shuffling, rhythmic joy of 'The Only One I Know' which filled the dance floor with boys with bowl cuts and girls who liked boys with bowl cuts. Missing that, and The Charlatans at that crucial moment, is one of my biggest regrets.

Perhaps the band who best defined my own relationship with Madchester were the Inspiral Carpets. In the summer of 1989 I walked into the McDonald's on Kirkcaldy High Street, filled out an application form to become a crew member and then headed home. I was sixteen and the income from a paper round, delivering the local free newspaper The Fife Leader, was no longer sufficient to provide for my ever maturing tastes. Sure a couple of pounds (literally) for dropping a couple of hundred free newspapers through the doors of my neighbourhood helped keep me in fizzy pop and sweets but it couldn't stretch to copies of both the NME and the Melody Maker or to buying the records being recommended inside them. I had no choice. I had to get a job.

A few days later I was called back to the restaurant to be interviewed in order to assess my suitability to cook processed meat, drop frozen French fries into a deep fat fryer and interact with the public. Despite my not being in possession of any previous processed meat, deep fat frying or dealing with other human beings experience I was given a job.

Incredible.

My rate of pay was somewhere around £2.50 an hour.

I could only work on Saturdays because my religious beliefs prohibited working on the Sabbath and that meant that I was

---

5. I wish this wasn't true, but it very definitely is.

restricted to a maximum weekly wage of about £20. We were paid fortnightly and, as long as I worked an eight hour shift each Saturday, I was banking about £40, which was enough for all the fizzy pop, sweets, crisps, music papers and records my acne ridden face could cope with.

After a year of McDonald's life I had bagged all of the gold stars for my badge[6], had been promoted to the position of lobby host and children's party host and was a well-established, if not well liked, member of the team. I also had a much larger record collection and, thanks to the fact that my diet consisted mainly of the junk food I was serving up to the public and sugar based treats purchased with my wages for doing so, my face looked like a dot-to-dot picture. A pus filled, red, swollen, disgusting dot-to-dot picture.

It was 1990 and something was changing in the pages of the NME and the Melody Maker. The back combed hair, long coats, quiffs and misery that had been the mainstay of both journals throughout the 1980s were slowly beginning to give way to something very different. Something that had more of a loose fit. Something baggier. Something more optimistic. Something that was built on pills and thrills and, well, you know the rest.

This was Madchester.

The rain coated lovers of eighties indie had been replaced, almost overnight, by 24 hour party people.

In the staff room at McDonald's, one kid was hip to this new beat.

His name was Michael[7] and he had the haircut, the flared jeans, the attitude and the record collection to put him right at the heart

---

6. I can no longer remember what each of the stars was for but I do know that one required you to know all of the qualities of a good fry, this included them being golden in colour and lightly salted.

7. The name has been changed to protect the guilty, this guy really was horrible to me.

of this new scene. He was also a bit of a prick to me and I used to feel a bit sick in my stomach whenever he was scheduled to work the same shift as me. But, despite that, he was *cool*.

One day Michael arrived with a VHS tape of a gig by a band that I had heard of but that I hadn't actually heard. They were called Inspiral Carpets and their cow and 'Cool as F**k!' T-shirts seemed to be surgically attached to the other cool kids in town. I'm not sure how I managed to miss all of this, but I would wager it had a lot to do with my having no real friends and being utterly obsessed with The Smiths - what a waste of time that has proven to be.

He put the video into the player in the staff room while I was waiting to start my shift, and by the time 'Real Thing' had concluded I was hooked. It was brilliant - a frantic, frenzied, frenetic, flash of energy, attitude and madness that swept me off my feet. The swirl and swish of the organ, the relentless battering of the drums, the beat, beat, beat of the bass, the urgency of the guitars, the roar of the vocals. It was the best thing I had ever heard. But there was a problem: I didn't like Michael. He liked The Inspiral Carpets. I couldn't like the thing that he liked. Petty? You betcha.

Ultimately I decided that the Carpets were just too good to not give in to their charms.

I became a closet fan.

I bought the debut album 'Life' on cassette and listened to it constantly for months. 'Real Thing' I knew from the live video[8] and 'She Comes in the Fall' I knew from watching, almost on a loop, the live performance from the same video - the marching band, the bass line and the instruction to 'WAKE UP' made it a firm favourite.

By the time the second album, 'The Beast Inside' arrived in April 1991, I had given up on trying to keep my love of them

---

8. 21.7.90 was recorded at the G-Mex in Manchester

a secret. Still too in awe of The Smiths to give up on my quiff and Evans blouses I was, nevertheless, equally evangelical and passionate about these baggy virtuosos with a knack for delivering pop so perfect it could melt your heart. The first single 'Caravan' was more confident, more assured, more mature and more and more and more of everything that had come before.

Before their next album arrived I had left home to serve a mission for my Church. Between December 1991 and July 1992 I was knocking on doors, treading rain soaked streets, living on porridge oats and trying to convince other people that the things I believed could be things they believed too. It was a strange, unsettling, life changing, wonderful, miserable and, at times, genuinely depressing experience. What made it really difficult wasn't being separated from my family and friends, it was being unable to listen to music - unless it was hymns. I cannot tell you how awful that was, and it probably wouldn't make sense even if I could.

By the time I came home, baggy was dead.

Madchester had fallen under the weight of its own legends - drugs had destroyed the Happy Mondays, The Stone Roses were missing in action in a farmhouse in Wales or something, Blur were reinventing themselves as something very different, Flowered Up, New Fast Automatic Daffodils, Mock Turtles and the rest had all had their moment in the spotlight. It was over.

When 'This is How it Feels' had become a major hit single, reaching number 14 in the charts, things could have gone one of two ways for the Carpets - they could have become one hit wonders with their career forever defined by that one moment or they could just disappear, never to be heard from again.

But neither of those things happened. They had bigger hits than 'This is How it Feels' and they didn't disappear. The death of the scene that had spawned them didn't destroy them like it destroyed some other bands. Instead, in October 1992, they released 'Revenge of the Goldfish' which, despite the dreadful title and the even more dreadful cover art, was their best record yet. Spawning four top forty singles and positioning them as one of the biggest bands in the country again. The album was a rare example of one that is bigger, maybe even better, than the singles that came from it. Twelve tracks of dizzy wonder.

As Britpop was about to become both A thing and THE thing, the sensible thing for a band like the Carpets to do would have been to head for the hills, wait it out and then hope that when it was all over, when the dust had settled, that there might still be an audience for them. Britpop wasn't baggy. It wasn't the summer of love, neither the first one nor the second. The clothes were sharper, the sounds tighter and the drugs that fuelled it were not ecstasy and cannabis but the more arrogance inducing, Gordon Gecko approved cocaine and speed. What place was there in this world for the Carpets?

As it turned out there was a place for them.

They returned in March 1994 with 'Devil Hopping' and far from sounding out of place and out of time they sounded thrillingly relevant. It wasn't a Britpop record but it was an album that served as a reminder of the role of Madchester in paving the way, kicking down the doors and shifting the culture for the new breed.

Madchester may not have been the start of Britpop, not really, but there can be no doubt that thanks to the intervention of Geno Washington, the mayhem of the Mondays and the craft and guile of Tim Burgess, it provided the spark that would, in just a few years, light the flame of a cultural revolution.

Chapter 2

For The Strangers

Suede

Once upon a time nobody had ever heard of Suede and nobody even knew that they needed Suede. How could they? Then somebody deep inside the darkest reaches of the Melody Maker[1] offices decided that it would be a terrific idea to put a band nobody had heard of, and who hadn't even released a single recorded note of music, onto the front cover. Approximately five minutes after that edition of the paper hit the shelves of WH Smith's no self respecting box room rebel could imagine a life without Suede.

It was April 1992. It was the year that the world decided that Nirvana were the best thing in music - despite, you know, the lack of melodies or sex appeal[2]. There was whining, there was greasy hair, there were clothes that hadn't seen Daz in about six months but there was precious little glamour and even fewer songs loaded with the things that make your heart beat a little faster - sex, outsiderdom, drugs, hope and hopelessness, perversion and petrol.

The debut single from Suede, 'The Drowners', arrived in May 1992 and it was a statement of intent. A calling card. A challenge

---

1. Suede The Best New Band in Britain, Melody Maker, 25/04/1992
2. I'm playing to the crowd here, Nirvana were, obviously, quite wonderful and if those eyes of Cobain didn't have you going all weak at the knees then there was something wrong with you.

to the musical establishment. A line in the sand. A rallying call to the grotesque and lonely. Four minutes and ten seconds that could change your life, especially if you didn't actually have a life. As soon as I heard Brett Anderson sneer the opening line I knew that I needed nothing more. What more *could* you need? Rolling drums, glam rock guitar, a bass line that made you go all peculiar and then a demand for an illegal firearm. It was a bit like 'Smells Like Teen Spirit' except for the fact that Cobain and the gang only gave you the guns bit.

The cover[3] for 'The Drowners' caused a bit of a stir in my house as it was a naked lady! I wasn't the sort of boy who had a secret stash of naughty magazines under my mattress so this was genuinely the first time that a set of lady bosoms had been delivered surreptitiously into my home. I convinced myself that because the naked woman was covered in paint that this was, in actual fact, art and not just boobs.

Not since a certain gang of Manchester miserabilists[4] had released their debut single about a decade earlier, also housed in an erotic sleeve and also charged with a particular type of sex and sexuality, had music fans and the music industry been quite so excited. And as with that band, the hype proved to be entirely justified. Suede were, even at this early stage, the real deal.

In October 1992 I was lurking in the shadows of The Venue in Edinburgh, waiting for them to take to the stage. My girlfriend at that time had seen them in Glasgow the night before and hadn't slept since. The atmosphere inside that tiny venue was charged with excitement, anticipation, love and desire. I can remember

---

3. The image on the cover of the single was a naked woman (Veruschka), her body painted to look like a 1920's gangster complete with stubble and dressed in a zoot suit. The artwork was a collaboration between the band and designers Peter Barrett and Andrew Biscomb.
4. The Smiths debut single 'Hand in Glove' featured a naked George O'Mara on the cover.

what I was wearing: an oversized pair of Levi's, a Morrissey T-shirt underneath a green velour woman's blouse (calm down ladies) and the obligatory indie kid scuffed and battered DM boots.

The gig was unforgettable and, as with all truly unforgettable moments, I remember next to nothing about what happened. It was manic. It was frantic. It was brilliant. At one point Brett Anderson found his lace blouse ripped from his body and, before I really thought about what I was doing, I was up on the stage, removing my own blouse and handing it to him. It lasted about as long as his own did.

When the debut album was released the following March I was visiting my girlfriend in the nowhere town where she lived. Two nobodies in nowhere - the Suede demographic. We headed to the only record shop in town that wasn't a Woolworths and bought the most eagerly anticipated debut album since the last most eagerly awaited debut album. We then hurried back to her parents' house and sat together on the sofa poring over the lyric sheet as one glam rock, indie pop, sleazy bed track, sex and drug referencing slab of glam 'n' roll followed another. The singles were all present and correct but, to my ears then, and now, the stand out song was 'Pantomime Horse'. It's a heartbreaking, achingly sad and fabulously enigmatic pop song. It washes over you and leaves you with your head barely above water. Drowning. Gasping. Dying. Happy to be there.

My life, at this point, was a wreck and Suede were cutting me loose.

In the months that followed things took a downward spiral within the band as Brett Anderson and Bernard Butler began to drift apart. Fault lines emerged in their relationship that caused, ultimately, a bitter break-up that ended with Bernard leaving the band before the recording of their second album 'Dog Man Star' was even completed.

From such seemingly infertile soil came an album that can lay claim to being a contender for best of the decade. 'Dog Man Star' hit me like a kiss. I can still remember everything…

Sunlight floods into my room. It bathes my face in a golden glow. It should feel warm but I don't feel warm. I feel cold. As cold on the outside as I do on the inside.

I'm wrapped up in my duvet, cocooned. Trying to shield myself from the horrors of the real world. I have an awful feeling that the dull ache of my depression might be about to devour me.

I'm afraid.

Cold, alone and afraid.

I don't actually know that I'm depressed.

Not at that moment. It is only later, after other spells of melancholy and feeling maladjusted, that I am given a label from a doctor and a prescription. However, although I now realised what was 'wrong' with me, I still didn't know why I was feeling this way.

If I am honest with you, I don't really want to get into all that David Copperfield kind of crap[5] that may offer some explanation. It won't help me and it would simply bore you.

Let's move on.

Or away.

What I remember most about that time was the loneliness. It was my only companion.

That's a good line isn't it? I must have read it somewhere. Like the David Copperfield one earlier that I pinched from 'Catcher in the Rye'. You shouldn't plagiarise, there's always someone, somewhere, who will know. Ready to trip you up and then start laughing at the misfortune that they have imposed upon you.[6]

---

5. Catcher in the Rye, J.D Salinger
6. Cemetry Gates, The Smiths

All I could really focus on was the fact that it was all going to end eventually and that I would soon be back in my digs looking at four walls and trying to stop myself from thinking about anything other than those four walls.

The whole experience of being at university is measured out, in my mind, in bus stops and rain.

As ever, as always, as usual, solace arrived from strangers.

I lied a lot then - telling everyone that I was fine, acting like a person who was having fun, wearing masks. But deceit can't save you so...

I had to burn.

At least that version of myself.

'We Are The Pigs' didn't sound much like Suede.

The glam stomp and punk romp of the debut album had been replaced by something else. It was elegant. It was pop music of the sort only they could make. Sophisticated? Romantic? Tragic? All of that and more.

It was the 'we' in 'We Are The Pigs' that struck me. Suede, again, positioning themselves as a gang. A safe space before we knew what a safe space was, or why they were needed. It was another rallying call.

As I listened to the album, all of my senses heightened. I felt alive. I felt less alone. I felt the blood pulse through my body and warm me. I felt my heart beat. I felt like somebody, somewhere, somehow understood me. It had arrived just about 18 months after 'Suede' in October 1994 but in what is really no time at all everything had changed. The early arthouse, art school, anti-rock leanings of 1991-1993 had been erased by the arrival of a band from Manchester two months earlier. But we will come to that, and them, later.

I can't bleat hard enough or long enough about how perfect 'Dog Man Star' is. It has gathered a bit of a cult following in the years since its release, which is some consolation for the fact that, despite positive reviews in the press, it failed to have the same sort of commercial impact as the debut album.

It's worth noting too that 'Dog Man Star' contains, arguably, the highlight of the singles released by Suede: 'The Wild Ones'. A song so perfect that it might actually be the son, or daughter, of whichever God you happen to believe in. I don't believe in any God and I still think it's perfect. I played it to a girl I liked once and she described it as 'Alright'. That ended the relationship.

But despite the brilliance of the album the elephant in the room was the fact that Butler was gone. Lauded as the spiritual heir to Johnny Marr and hailed by chin stroking musos everywhere as a genius, he was history. For the indier than thou of the British music world this was the equivalent of Robbie leaving Take That.

Butler himself has said that leaving was a 'mistake', telling Scottish tabloid The Daily Record that *'when I left Suede I didn't do it because I fell out with people. I did it because I didn't want the producer we had to mix an album. It was a case of call my bluff. It was him or me. It was a stupid mistake. I was stupid enough to go for it. It shouldn't have gone that far.'*[7]

That 'mistake' could very easily have been the end of Suede. What nobody could have envisaged was the arrival of a barely pubescent guitar player and songwriter called Richard Oakes. A musician whom Brett Anderson had informed us was 'going to blow our heads off.' The public, and the press, were less than convinced. In footballing terms this was like selling a Maradona and replacing him with a Francis Jeffers[8]. This had disaster written all over it. For people who already hated the bisexual who had never had a homosexual experience (oh Brett) this was manna from heaven and the sniggering was loud and lengthy.

---

7. Daily Record, September 2002
8. Footballer given the moniker 'The fox in the box' despite not actually scoring all that often.

What we didn't know, what we couldn't have known, was that Brett was right and that little Richard was, indeed, about to blow us all away with his contributions to one of the best pop albums of the Britpop era.

'Trash' was the lead single and the first fruits of the Anderson/ Oakes songwriting partnership to be presented to the public. It brought the sniggering to a shuddering halt as it not only raced to number three in the charts but became their biggest selling single as a result. Rather than kill Suede, the departure of Butler had seen them born again, hallelujah, praise be etc.

The first fruits of that Anderson/Oakes partnership were the songs that would form the bulk of the ten tracks on 'Coming Up'.

'Trash', 'Filmstar', 'She', 'Beautiful Ones', 'Picnic by the Motorway' and 'Saturday Night' were little Dickie's six contributions to the album. That makes four top ten singles written for your debut album - each one a shuddering, slinky, sexy, sassy, slice of glam/pop brilliance. All before he left his teens. Did somebody say 'genius'?

Where 'Dog Man Star' had been a gothic glory, 'Coming Up' was the sound of a band doing exactly that - having been gasping, dying and yet somehow still alive after the rush and the push of fame and its intoxicating but fatal flames over the previous four years. The departure of Butler and the arrival of Oakes and, crucially, of the elegantly inelegant Neil Codling had rejuvenated the band and their sound.

Many of the themes and much of the imagery remains resolutely Suede-ish but it shimmers and shines in a way that their previous work had not. It was as though someone had opened the curtains at Suede towers and, arguably for the first time, sunlight had bathed them in a golden glow.

It went to number one in the UK charts and was a hit in several other countries around the world. Indeed, it would eventually go platinum here in the UK and elevated the band from the biggest indie band in the country to a genuine household name, with everyone from 'jumble sale mums' and Sadies to young men and 'graffiti women' happily singing along to the likes of 'Beautiful Ones' and 'Trash'. One of the highlights of 'Coming Up' wasn't any of the singles though, but rather the penultimate track 'The Chemistry Between Us'. It's a hymn to wasteland youth, adolescent yearning and teenage daydreams - with some drug references thrown in for good measure.

Who hasn't been young and easily led? Who was ever tired of being young? Nobody. Well, not me anyway. I loved being young. I was too boring for anyone ever to have wanted to lead me anywhere - but I'd have gone if I'd been asked. Gladly. Happily. Easily.

Suede were now back and they were bigger, better and bolder than ever. The world was their oyster. World tours. Stadium gigs. Awards. It was all just around the corner. Farewell indie disco and hello to the big time.

And then came 'Head Music'.

Suede decided to reveal the title for their fourth studio album one letter at a time, one week apart.

H.

E.

'It's going to be 'Heroin' isn't it?' squealed expectant fans and journalists.

Those naughty Suede boys.

Playing fast and loose with the rumours about Brett's drug use at this time.

Then Mat Osman told the NME that the album would, in fact, be called 'Head Music'.

I know that 'Heroin' would have been a cliché but it would also have been a nice nod to the Velvet Underground and a call back to 'Heroine' from 'Dog Man Star' so I was a bit disappointed.

What none of us knew for certain, but many suspected, was that at that time heroin was playing a fairly major role in Suede World during the run up to the recording of 'Head Music'.

'More than anything, there started to be a whole load of people he was associating with, who I just couldn't stand. They had nothing to do with the band, nothing to do with anything but drugs. They were drug buddies.'[9]

'Buddies' like this can be poison to a band.

At one point in time I was friends with a well-known musician with world tours, stadiums, hit singles and all the rest of it. Life was good for him. Then he found some 'buddies' who were not part of the music scene - parasites is what they were. They saw him as a potential cash cow. To keep him close they drip, drip, dripped poison in his ear about other people in the band, feeding his ego and fuelling resentments that, ultimately, didn't end well. I can well imagine the influence of Brett's drug 'buddies'.

Parasites.

'Electricity', released in April 1999, the lead single from 'Head Music' sounded like 'Filmstar', 'Trash' and 'The Beautiful Ones' from 'Coming Up'. It was resolutely, defiantly Suede. Violent homes, lips like pain, AC/DC and kissing all yelped and howled by Brett while Richard's guitars did something similar. Was familiarity in danger of breeding contempt? While 'Electricity' is a great pop song it left me feeling perhaps let down? No. Not let down, but looking for, waiting for, something more. A return to the grandeur of 'Dog Man Star' maybe? Or perhaps a great leap forward of some sort? This wasn't either of those things, it was the sound of a band treading water, playing it safe...

The album itself arrived a month later and it was a mixed bag. Neither bad nor genius. There were moments when they sounded

---

9. Matt Osman, 'Love and Poison' by David Barnett, 2003

better than they ever had and moments when they sounded finished, bored and creatively dead.

That hadn't ever seemed like something one would ever be able to say about Suede but when the follow up to 'Head Music' arrived it was clear that whatever magic had created three of the greatest albums of the nineties had, like a magician's assistant, disappeared.

The band, and Anderson in particular, have always rejected any and all connection to Britpop. Speaking in 2019 he said *'I disassociated myself from that (Britpop) very early on, as I saw what I saw as becoming this kind of laddish, jingoistic, cartoon happening, which became Britpop, I very quickly distanced Suede from that.'*[10]

And so it came to pass that there was much wailing and gnashing of teeth.

Largely from people who don't really understand what Britpop is, or was, and who haven't really read what Brett Anderson had to say about it.

It is dangerous to conflate Britpop with Cool Britannia as they are two very different things. One was a lazy, all encompassing scene created by music journalists and the other was a term created and weaponised by political figures to achieve power and set an agenda.

'Cool Britannia' was a branding exercise, an attempt to shift attitudes and to drag Britain from the place of self-loathing and near fecklessness that it had drifted into thanks to the economic strife of the eighties and the worst aspects of Thatcherism - it was, in many ways, Harry Enfield's 'Loadsamoney' come to life. That wasn't the actual intention of course - the true objective was to foster creative energy, entrepreneurial capitalism and national

---

10. BBC Hardtalk, 2019

pride in order to re-energise the country and put Britain centre stage globally.

It worked.

The problem was that an integral part of Cool Britannia was the rise of lad culture (for men and women) and a blizzard of cocaine which, if we are all being honest, isn't a drug that makes people more pleasant and which also created a space where national pride could, all too easily, slip into jingoism.

When Brett Anderson describes his discomfort with laddism, jingoism and blatant misogyny he is speaking for me. However, although Brett sees those things as being directly linked to Britpop - I don't.

Britpop was never a genre.

There isn't a Britpop sound.

One would struggle to describe the 'look' of a Britpop band.

Bands didn't even have to be British to be Britpop.

Britpop was really indie gone mainstream.

It is difficult to see it as being jingoistic when it includes the likes of Eels (American), The Wannadies (Sweden), The Cardigans (Sweden), Ash (Irish) or when it has key voices who were black and Asian. Tricky too to see it as being misogynistic when some of the most successful and revered writers and musicians of the era were women like Justine Frischmann, Louise Wener and Sonya Madan. Challenging to see it as laddish when characters like Jaime Harding, Mark Morriss, Patrick Duff and others were stars, each of them writing openly, honestly and passionately about affairs of the heart, domestic violence, heartache and more.

Yes, many of the bands who fall under the Britpop umbrella flirted with classic, iconic, British imagery, or more accurately Mod iconography, but none of them were flirting with fascism or waving the Union Jack as means of making a political comment. This was all style and very little substance.

It isn't my place to even consider correcting someone like Brett Anderson who is, let us be honest, my superior in almost every way that one could imagine but I do think that it is inaccurate, possibly disingenuous, to see Britpop in such negative terms or as being wholly unpleasant.

Brett is, of course, right to seek to disassociate himself, and his band, from any label or genre that he sees as being out of step with his ethos, his philosophy, his politics and in so doing he has remained true to the things that made Suede one of the most important bands of the nineties.

Chapter 3

British Image #1

Blur

Across 1990 and 1991, a band of Madchester inspired, middle-class Southern boys enjoyed a little bit of chart success and lot of press coverage - the former due to the records being a little bit good (but not much more than that) and the latter being down to their frontman owning a mouth that was turbo-charged and a face that was just too pretty. They were Blur and they were the dictionary definition of 'alright'.

Their first single 'She's So High' was, officially, a double A-side with 'I Know'. I doubt that anyone who listened to the woozy, fuzzy and ever so slightly shoegaze-y 'She's So High' really believed that this was the work of a band who would go on to define an entire era. It is a lovely little pop song, but nothing more than that. Despite bringing the band to the attention of the music press, 'She's So High' failed to make its way into the top forty, and it wouldn't have been unreasonable to think that they had peaked. But then they released 'There's No Other Way', a bona fide pop gem that thrust them into the mainstream. It's another stab at the psychedelic sounds of baggy era Manchester and it still fills floors at indie discos up and down the country - it's just that now the people dancing have swapped their bowl cuts for male pattern baldness.

What is most interesting about 'There's No Other Way' though is not the song but the accompanying video. It starts with a worm winding its way through the grass, before two girls, twins dressed in identical clothes, play catch in the garden where there is a row of daffodils while from behind a window Damon Albarn watches all of this with a look of detachment on his face. The influence and inspiration are obviously the opening moments of David Lynch's macabre, nightmarish, masterpiece 'Blue Velvet' meeting Kubrick's 'The Shining' in an English country garden. Once those unsettling moments are over, we find ourselves inside the family home with a traditional English roast dinner being served up. Damon looks straight at the camera looking like a Droog with a pudding bowl haircut - interestingly, it isn't the last time that Damon will use that imagery. What this all says is that Blur were pop culture vultures. Like Lloyd Cole and the Commotions singing about 'On the Waterfront' or Morrissey using 'A Taste of Honey' as the basis for much of his early canon, Blur were looking outside tattered copies of 'Rubber Soul' for inspiration.

Then came a third single, 'Bang'. 'Bang' is just *fine*. It is a song that brings a smile to your face when it pops up on shuffle and it has you singing along like a loon but I'm not sure anyone ever seeks it out, not even Blur. It feels a bit under-cooked, unfinished, rushed and maybe, just maybe, a little bit lazy. One of the b-sides 'Luminous' is a much more interesting proposition but it couldn't ever have been a single as it is too dense, too dark, too brooding. It hints at who Blur could have become had they decided the future was Chapterhouse.

In August 1991 the band released their debut album 'Leisure'. Britain was a place where Ian Brown had replaced the Queen as the (un)official (out of our) Head of State. Shaun William Ryder was the people's poet laureate. People were flowered up. Everybody knew that this was how it feels. Everything had gone a bit baggy, soft around the edges, dreamy and trippy. Not for me. I was a slightly, actually very, repressed teenage boy in a coastal town of the sort that Sir John Betjeman would weep over. Come friendly bombs and fall on Kirkcaldy. It doesn't scan very well, but it was a far better target for a full blown nuclear assault than Slough. At least that was how it seemed to me.

Nirvana were about to become a thing. Both 'Smells Like Teen Spirit' and 'Nevermind' were looming. The summer of love would soon be over. Anger, discontent, dreadful clothes and even worse hair was on the horizon. Blur, it seemed, were a band out of time. Their moment had, perhaps, already passed.

Often ignored because of the era defining nature of 'Modern Life is Rubbish', the global smash of 'Parklife' and then the genre hopping, increasingly mature and endlessly creative follow up work, it is the 'lost' Blur album, or at least the one that people talk least about. What is interesting about 'Leisure' though is that there are moments on it where you can hear what was to come later. It is the sound of a band crafting, creating, honing and finding their identity. Take 'Repetition' which could be the demo version of 'Oily Water' or 'Pressure on Julian' from 'Modern Life is Rubbish' with its hazy, fuzzy, muggy sound and the deployment of a megaphone for Damon to intone 'slow down don't be so eager to let me go'. The same could be said for 'Come Together' which also sounds like a template for some of those 'Modern Life...' tracks.

'Leisure' isn't a perfect album, far from it, and it doesn't sit anywhere near the top table of Blur's catalogue but it cannot simply be dismissed, because it does a good job of introducing the band and pointing us in the direction that they would head next. Two great singles along with four songs that stand up against anything else that comes after make 'Leisure' an album worth revisiting.

A truly miserable experience on a tour of America changed Damon Albarn, changed Blur and, ultimately, changed British popular culture. Albarn had looked around and had been terrified by what he had seen in America. Taking a 'baggy' album to a country where grunge was the dominant musical form they were lost, out of place and close to breaking. Fearing that something vital could be lost forever by the Coca-Colanisation of popular culture from America, Blur began the process of positioning themselves as some sort of cultural Home Guard on their return. This wasn't about jingoism or xenophobia, it was about a desire to protect the things they valued in British pop, to be a barrier against the tsunami of grunge that was threatening to wipe everything else out. They had to do *something*.

That something was 'Popscene'. Three minutes and fifteen seconds of psychedelic guitar, furious drumming, louche bass and lyrics that were spat out with a laid back fury. It was a punk-pop blast of brilliance that made the earlier releases seem like a twisted practical joke. The problem was that the world wasn't listening. It charted lower than either 'There's No Other Way' and 'Bang' making it look like this was a brilliant full stop to a less than brilliant career.

Scurrying off to the studio to lick their wounds, the band embarked on a recording session that would result in one of the finest albums ever released by a British band. A record that would put British music and British musicians centre stage on the world stage. A record that would have as much impact on fashion as it would on music. A record that would be the start of their path to becoming the biggest band in the country.

Where 'Popscene' had sounded like a burst of righteous indignation, a song determined to let the world know how angry they were at being overlooked in favour of people in dreadful clothes and with even more dreadful hair, the album that followed was the sound of a band, and Damon Albarn in particular, trying to figure out their place in the world, to understand their identity and to see if they could find a reason to take some pride in their country's cultural heritage. The result was 'Modern Life is Rubbish'.

Meanwhile, I was holed up in my bedroom with a copy of 'The World Won't Listen' by The Smiths playing on a loop on my cassette player. My parents were slowly being driven mad. I had cultivated the finest quiff in the land and I had excluded nearly all other music from my life. The exceptions to this were the bands that my dad loved: he had been an original Mod back in the swinging sixties, man and about 50% of my collection of LPs were his old Who, Small Faces, Kinks and Jam records along with a healthy smattering of Motown. Despite my love of Morrissey I just couldn't get on board with the Elvis and rockabilly thing as there was too much grease in the hair and 'Grease' in the air.

I used to rush down to John Menzies on Kirkcaldy High Street every Wednesday after school to pick up my copies of NME and Melody Maker. Thumbing through one of them I stumbled across a picture of Blur. They looked very different to the way they had 12 months ago. Fred Perry shirts, three button suit jackets, desert boots and docs - they were skinheads with mop tops. Behind them the wall was sprayed with graffiti saying 'British Image 1'. I was smitten. My parents had both been Mods in the sixties and so I instantly got what Blur were invoking and I wanted in on whatever it was that they were doing.

Clemenceau once said: 'A patriot loves his own country, a nationalist hates everyone else's'. Some would argue that there is precious little difference between patriotism and nationalism but I do like the idea of love of one's own country and I very much don't like the idea of hating someone else's. There are lots of things about Britain that I love: cricket, good manners, respect and respectability, the language, the eccentrics, football on a Saturday and roast beef on a Sunday, queuing, Wimbledon, strawberries and cream, the weather, green and pleasant land and on and on I could go. The more cynical (maybe more enlightened) can dismiss this as romantic guff if you like, but I likes a bit of romance.

This image of Blur and the accompanying music all spoke to me in a very real way. In a way that the likes of Cobain and Vedder hadn't been able to. The music they played said nothing to me about my life. 'Modern Life is Rubbish' though *became* my life. The album was preceded by a single 'For Tomorrow', which came housed in a sleeve that looked like a boy's birthday card from the post-war years. A cloudy sky with silhouetted Spitfires making their way home and a bright red Blur badge in the top left hand corner. It was vintage before vintage was a 'thing'. It was retro from the get-go.

'Modern Life is Rubbish' is more than an album. It is a manifesto. It is a rejection of the modern world. It is a loving nod to a past that may never have existed. It is a blueprint for what should come next. What 'Modern Life...' offered was a vision of England's past that while romantic, idealised and inaccurate in many ways was, nevertheless, quite beautiful. Beauty was not a word that featured prominently in anyone's dialogue throughout the grunge era. At the same time, Blur seemed to be suggesting that there was no reason why we all couldn't celebrate the best of Britain and Britishness without the need for jingoism or narrow xenophobia. From the perfection of 'For Tomorrow' to the trippy delights of 'Resigned' and all the pop, punk and new wave delights in between, it is a staggering and defiant work. Only ears made of cloth and a heart of stone could fail to appreciate it.

'It's an album that nearly didn't get made,' says its producer and, maybe, unofficial fifth member of the band, Stephen Street. 'I had produced about a third of 'Leisure' but Dave Balfe at Food didn't want me for the next one. Then a chance meeting with Graham Coxon at a Cranberries gig rekindled his memories of working with me, he mentioned it to Damon and then I got a call about the possibility of working with them again. It wasn't a huge success but it tapped into the zeitgeist. It was the stepping stone for what would happen with 'Parklife'.

Shortly after the album's release, word reached my provincial ears about a gig that Blur were going to be playing in Glasgow. As part of the Yamaha sponsored 'Music Quest' (no sniggering at the back there) they would be playing a set that was going to be recorded for broadcast at a later date by Radio 1. I managed to secure a couple of tickets for me and my best friend Chris, and off we went. We drove to Glasgow in a dilapidated Lada that had been bought for Chris as a 'reward' for passing his exams a few years earlier. It had more in common with the vehicle that Fred Flintstone pedals to work than any modern car. Quite how it made it beyond the end of my road never mind all the way to Glasgow is beyond me - but it did.

The line-up for the Music Quest included Candy Ranch, the regional winners of the battle of the bands competition of the same name. Their lead singer wore a top hat which, I'm afraid to say, marked their card with Chris and I. I once saw Chris beat up a poor unfortunate who had made a snide comment about his desert boots, so his tolerance for poor sartorial choices or commentary was very low.

Thankfully, Chris was diverted from physically tackling the singer of Candy Ranch by the arrival of the second band of the night. That we were witnessing Blur and Radiohead on the same bill seems, now, to be incredible but it is made more so by the fact that the cost of the ticket was seven pounds. This shows that on Friday 3 September 1993, the sort of music that would, in just twelve months, be dominating the charts and leading a pop cultural revolution was still, very much, a fringe event.

This was in fact the last night of the 'Modern Life is Rubbish' UK tour but in a world without the internet none of us knew what to expect. Blur took to the stage in front of a set that was dressed to look like a sitting room, with all of the furniture blown up to epic proportions. It was ace. A huge standard lamp towered by the drum kit. There was an oversized armchair. I may be dreaming but I seem to recall a fake cooker and a fridge. Who knows. Who cares? All that mattered was that I was there. It wasn't quite the Sex Pistols at the Manchester Free Trade Hall, but I'm willing to bet that the couple of hundred punters who had turned out to see Blur that night all felt the same way as me - that this was the start of *something*.

Even with the feeling that we had been witness to something special that night, I don't think that any of us, certainly not me, really imagined that Blur were set to do what they did next and become the biggest band in the country.

STEPHEN STREET[1]: *'After we did 'Modern Life is Rubbish', I saw them playing the tent at Reading festival and there was a real buzz that day, you could really tell something was happening. The image was so strong, the chemistry between them on stage was so strong. I felt a lot of affection for them. When we did 'Parklife' I wanted to make sure it was great, I didn't want them to fall by the wayside again.'*

Like all of the great bands, Blur weren't interested in standing still. They didn't want to repeat what they had already done, they wanted to move on, try new things, get bigger and reach more people. There was a drive and ambition in the band that was matched only by their ability.

In my digs at university, I was lying on the floor listening to the Evening Session on Radio 1. The Evening Session was a bit like the John Peel show but for people who didn't understand The Fall. Hosts Jo Whiley and Steve Lamacq played music with recognisable melodies from bands people had heard of. Horses for courses. They were about to give the new single from Blur its first play. It was called 'Girls and Boys' and I was poised over

---

1. Legendary record producer who worked with several Britpop bands.

the tape deck, ready to hit record and play simultaneously so that I could listen to it again later.

I don't get it.

It didn't sound like 'Modern Life is Rubbish'.

It didn't sound like The Kinks or The Jam or The Smiths or any of the 'right' bands.

It sounded *weird*. Squelchy with bleeps and beats. I didn't like it. Not at all. I disliked it so much that I left the house and walked to the nearest payphone to call Chris. I was sure he would have been listening. When he answered I said 'Did you hear it?' and he replied 'Aye, it was shite.' Peter Ustinov, Chris was not.

I trudged back to my room and flopped on the bed. Then, just to prove that I was right, I rewound the tape and hit play. Then again. By the third play I realised that I had made a terrible mistake. This wasn't terrible, it was the greatest thing I've ever heard. It's all light on the surface but underneath lurks something darker. Like 'Colin Zeal' or 'Pressure on Julian' from 'Modern Life is Rubbish' this is social commentary through character study and further evidence that Damon Albarn's near absolute belief in his own talent might not be misplaced or mistaken.

When 'Girls and Boys' arrived I bought it on cassette, only because it came packaged like a packet of condoms. This, to a boy who was trying his very best to stick, rigidly, to his religion's teachings on nakedness and naughtiness with ladies, was positively outrageous. It reached number five in the charts - the band's highest placing to date. The top ten that week included Mariah Carey, Bruce Springsteen, Tori Amos and M-People - legends and genuine pop stars, along with Eurobeat stars like Reel 2 Reel. This felt like a really big deal - here was an indie band knocking around the top end of the charts along with people who sold records by the millions and not by the dozen.

What is curious about the success of 'Girls and Boys' and consequently of 'Parklife', was that the audience remained the same. Gigs on the tour were raucous, celebratory and sold out but the crowds were made up almost entirely of the same sorts of people you had always found following indie bands. Even though they had flirted with Mod and skinhead style and were now taking the football casuals of the mid-80s as the inspiration for their wardrobe, they, and their audience, were still mercifully free of the darker attributes of any of those scenes. They were dandies in Tacchinni, fops in Ellesse. You can view it as cultural tourism or as a loving homage but you have to appreciate their ability to rein in any hint of what would now be seen as toxic masculinity.

However, even the terrace stomp of 'Parklife' with rent-a-geezer Phil Daniels on vocals and a pint of beer on the front cover didn't find them favour with the Bloke Army who were about to stage an assault on the indie music scene that would, ultimately, end this first period of Britpop. The reason for this was the fact that Blur and a lot of the other 'first wave' Britpop bands embraced elements of camp, baroque and music hall. While there were, very clearly, songs that had heart and soul, that traded in the reality of life in poetic, sometimes shocking, ways there was also a great deal of humour and pretence. While Damon may not have flirted with sex and sexuality in the same way as Brett Anderson or Jarvis Cocker he was, undeniably, a bit too fey to ever be taken seriously as 'one of the lads'. Crucially, he wouldn't have wanted to be.

'Parklife' quickly became the album of the year on its release in April 1994 and it spawned another two singles, the lush, cinematic 'To The End' which, backstage at the Queen's Hall in Edinburgh, Damon assured me was going to be a number one record (it peaked at number sixteen in the UK) and 'End of a Century'. It was now official - Blur were pop stars. They were on the cover of every magazine, they were on every radio and television show you could think of and they were draped on the walls of boys and girls, girls and boys, across the country.

Outside the Plaza in Glasgow in May 1994, Chris and I were contemplating whether or not our decision to arrive at the venue about four hours before the doors opened had been a mistake when the stage door opened and a well dressed young man approached us to ask if there were any good second hand record stores in town. This was Paul Tunkin, the official tour DJ, a position bestowed upon him as the creator of the hippest hang out in London, Blow Up!. Blow Up! was *the* club in London. It was where the coolest kids gathered to dance to the coolest sounds - soundtracks, soul, Mod, indie and, now, Britpop. I didn't actually know about any of that at this point because I hadn't been, but I had heard about it. Chris and I offered to take Paul into town in search of records for his set before that night's gig. Two things happened as a result of this: firstly, we were placed on the guest lists and given backstage passes for both that night's show and the one the following night in Edinburgh. This meant that after the show we found ourselves sitting with Damon Albarn despite the fact that he wasn't doing a very good job of being a pop star and was, instead, doing a very good impression of being a record company accountant as he told us all about the target demographic for 'To The End'. At the other end of the room I could see Louise Wener of Sleeper surrounded by a small group of very pretty girls and I was struck by the fact that I had made a terrible choice.

The second consequence of being willing to take Paul to find records was that we were also able to blag our way into the after show party on the last night of the tour, which took place at the Alexandra Palace in London, where Blur were supported by acid jazz hip cats Corduroy, some teenagers called Supergrass and the kitchen sink drama of Pulp. That show took place in October and it possibly acts as the last hurrah of the first phase of Britpop before everything went a bit lad shaped. The show itself was a glorious celebration of British pop music at that moment in time. Corduroy sounded like the house band for a 'happening' in a flat on Carnaby

Street sometime in 1966, a fusion of soul, funk and jazz that even managed to drag something like dancing out of the ordinarily awkward likes of me in the crowd. Supergrass wouldn't release their debut single 'Caught By The Fuzz' until ten days after this show but they were a riot, like a shot of dextroamphetamine with sideburns. Pulp were just Pulp, with Jarvis Cocker determined to make the most of this moment and put himself exactly where he believed he should be, in the charts and on the telly.

Many people see Knebworth and Oasis dragging a quarter of a million people to a field in England as the high point of Britpop, but it wasn't, not really. It was a big deal and so were Oasis but Britpop wasn't about big deals, it was about craft, guile, wit, style and camp. That's why Blur at the Ally Pally is the real high point of Britpop. We were given a bingo card so that we could win a night with Blur (everyone won), it took place in an iconic venue in London, it celebrated the camp history of British popular culture with the use of 'Getta Bloomin' Move On (The Self Preservation Society)' from 'The Italian Job' as Blur's entry music and the crowd was made up of kids dressed in sharp suits and Biba style dresses. Blur went on to play bigger gigs to bigger crowds but nothing that captured the mood or the moment quite like this.

By the time the Brit Awards for 1995 happened, Blur and Oasis were a big deal. They filled column inches in the tabloids, the broadsheets and the music press without really doing anything. They were pop stars. Girls and boys adored them.

'Definitely Maybe' had sold enough copies to make sure that every person on the planet was never more than 3 feet away from one while at the same time 'Parklife' had turned Blur into the biggest pop band in the world.

Heady times.

When Blur won the award for best band in the face of stiff competition from Eternal, M-People, Pink Floyd and Oasis, Damon Albarn said 'I think this should have been shared with

Oasis' with Graham Coxon chiming in with 'Much love and respect to them.' Author of the weighty Britpop era tome 'The Last Party', John Harris said of this, '*I never knew if he was joking*' but a look at the video of the night shows that neither Albarn nor Coxon looked smug or like they are poking fun at anyone and even Alex James mentioned Oasis in his remarks as they picked up the gong. At this point it looked like there was some, perhaps grudging, respect between the two groups.

That's how it may have seemed to nice boys like Blur but for the slightly rougher, tougher and harder lads from Oasis the feeling was very far from mutual. As 1995 wound on public confrontations and private resentments began to grow ever more frequent and ever more hostile. The nadir of these skirmishes arrived later in the year when Noel said that he hoped both Albarn and James would catch AIDS and die. For a man who is ready with ready wit at any time this was a rare example of vulgarity. He retracted the statement but it cast a long shadow over the interactions between the bands for a long while after.

The cold war was over.

Things were about to become very hot.

Scorching.

Sizzling.

Fiery.

Both bands (and both labels depending on which version of events you prefer) decided to go head to head, to step out into the no man's land of the charts and release singles on the same day.

For each band there was a desire to defend their own islands of pop, whatever the cost may be, and they were ready to fight on the shelves of HMV, on the radio stations of provincial towns, in the fields of rural England, on the High Streets of Scotland, with neither prepared to countenance the idea of surrender.

If there was going to be a war it was vital that each band chose their weapons carefully in order to ensure victory.

Blur have had twenty-six top forty singles.

Twenty-six.

The song they chose to release in their battle for number one against Oasis, and to secure what they believed would be a conclusion to hostilities was 'Country House'.

'Country House'.

A song so dreadful that it makes 'Mr Blobby' sound like 'Love Will Tear Us Apart' by comparison. It's a novelty record. A comedy song.

This wasn't the first time that Blur had chosen a song like this as a single. 'Parklife' was just as bad. Both were the sort of thing that should have been secreted away on a b-side to something better. The fact that neither was can, I think, be attributed to Damon Albarn believing his own hype at this point.

'Country House' also came with one of the worst music videos in the history of the medium, a weirdly sexist 'homage' to the even weirder and even more sexist Benny Hill. The best way to describe this whole thing is *tacky*.

Blur were better than this.

Their forthcoming album 'The Great Escape' had many songs that would have been better singles -actually, *every* song on 'The Great Escape' would have been a better choice for a single than this. Including that one with Ken Livingstone[2] on it.

Lots of people have been equally critical of the choice that Oasis made, 'Roll with It' and have used words like 'lumpen' to describe it. It's true that it, like 'Country House', is far from being prime cut Oasis but, by comparison with 'Country House' it sounds positively epic.

Tim Burgess, who knows a thing or two about writing pop songs, described 'Roll With It' as *'flat pack Oasis'* and it's true. If No-Way-Sis had released this as a single when they inexplicably

---

2. Former Mayor of London

secured a record deal, people would have laughed their socks off at their brazenness.

But, crucially, it wasn't as awful as 'Country House' and it seemed obvious which song would reach the top of the pops at the end of the week.

I bought 'Country House'. In fact, I bought it on all three formats.

You see, I had naively decided that Blur were a Mod band, and in the heat and general giddiness of Britpop I thought that I was a Mod too. I have no idea why I thought either thing but that's the truth of it. I saw Oasis as something else.

Thanks to the extra CD single that Blur were able to offer thanks to having the might of a major label behind them, they found themselves at number one in the charts at the end of the week.

They really knocked Oasis out.

The battle was over.

Blur were victorious.

Oasis were left to return to camp with their noses bloodied, their egos knocked, their pride bruised but, crucially, they were still standing.

Following the battle for the number one spot, Oasis mounted an offensive campaign that left Blur reeling and that ultimately put them into a different league when it came to the traditional measures of success in the music business, such as record sales, tour revenues, wider public recognition and acceptance.

'(What's the Story) Morning Glory' was to become one of the biggest selling albums by a British act ever, shifting, at the last count, nearly five million copies and going fourteen times platinum in the UK alone. It hit the number one spot in nine countries and broke the top ten in America.

'The Great Escape' by comparison, sold less than a million copies (still no mean feat) and reached the dizzying height of number one hundred and fifty in the US charts.

Of course the 'truth' does become more complicated and murky when discussion turns to which album is 'better' as that is all about personal taste. At the time of release I was, again, very definitely (no maybes) in team Blur. I saw 'The Great Escape' as further evidence of the genius of everyone involved in its creation and even at the time I found 'Morning Glory' to be a bit, well, boring?

The war was over.

Oasis had won.

They were the biggest band in Britain.

They were one of the biggest bands in the world.

They had left their contemporaries from Britpop far behind and had delivered the sort of beating to Blur that could have finished other bands completely.

Blur though are not 'other' bands and Damon Albarn is nothing if not competitive, ambitious and convinced of his own talents even when others may doubt them - perhaps *especially* when others doubt them.

Graham Coxon had grown increasingly uncomfortable in the Britpop spotlight, and even more uncomfortable with things like 'Country House' and its accompanying video. He wanted to move things on, experiment, stretch, and change direction.

Not for the first time Blur decided to do the very thing that nobody expected of them and just as they had ditched the baggy clothes and Madchester-lite sound following 'Leisure' they now turned their back on the Mockney affectations and delivered an album every bit as culturally important as 'Modern Life Is Rubbish' had been back in 1993.

While Pulp's 'This is Hardcore' had been the sound of the end of the Britpop party, it was still very much a recognisably 'Pulp' sounding record. Meanwhile, Blur's eponymous fifth album was the end of the Britpop sound. It was a dark, brooding, intense and, at times, lo-fi album. The lead single 'Beetlebum' jettisoned the light and pop touch of the Britpop trilogy and plunged Blur fans into an entirely new sonic world - it is, frankly, a record that is soaked in misery; and it sounds wonderful because of it. The fact that it delivered a second number one single was evidence of how the world had shifted in the months since 'The Great Escape'. The very notion of a song like 'Beetlebum' shifting enough copies to reach the top spot in the charts even six months earlier would have been too fanciful to even imagine.

Better was to come as they then unleashed 'Song 2' which was the sort of song the likes of Nirvana thought they were recording during the grunge era but which they had neither the talent nor the imagination to realise. It's a riotous, ramshackle, rowdy two minutes and one second of fire and fury. Coxon hammers the melody like some sort of Norse God pounding on the doors of Valhalla (you know the one I mean - big bloke, hammer, Australian) and Albarn unleashes a sneering vocal and near nonsensical lyrics. It's perfect in every way.

That was it.

Blur gave up on being the biggest pop band in the world, as after all they had achieved that already and had found it didn't quite agree with them, and focused instead on being one of the finest bands ever. Each album bringing a new sound while always remaining resolutely Blur.

Damon decided to have another go at the pop star thing but this time from behind the curtain with Gorillaz. A mad hybrid of anime, graffiti art, comic book creation, pop, soul, funk and hip-hop. Incredibly, he pulled it off and a band who didn't really exist sold lorry loads of records and played sold out concerts to adoring fans. Then when he got bored with that, he wrote operas and dabbled in world music.

Graham Coxon has released eight solo albums and in the process has cemented his position not just as a great guitarist but as a singer and songwriter in his own right. He also seems, and

I appreciate I have no way of knowing how true this is, to be happier than the frustrated boy [3] on the back of a tour bus on 'Star Shaped' or the one who threatened to fling himself out of a window during a drunken night at the height of the whole Blur v Oasis 'thing'. I hope so.

As for Dave and Alex -one makes cheese and one has dabbled in politics. I'd rather not get involved.

---

3. In 1993 a video called 'Star Shaped' was released, it captured Blur on, and off, stage across Europe and at one point Graham is filmed trying, unsuccessfully, to drink a cup of tea from a china cup. His frustrations are amplified by the fact that Alex James is managing the same task with no apparent difficulties.

Chapter 4

No Wonder You're Looking Thin

Pulp

'It's about a guy who's liking this girl who's a bit posh and, in a way, he's put off by some of her attitudes. That bit is true, I did meet this girl at St. Martins who was doing a different course and we are at a bar and she was going on about wanting to go and live in Hackney with the common people and I thought 'That's a bit much that innit.' but I did fancy her.'

(Jarvis Cocker, 2012)

A lot of people really love 'Common People'. It is, for them, a reminder of their youth. It has become the Britpop national anthem. It evokes memories of the sunny, hopeful, optimistic nineties. It is the soundtrack to heady nights on the dance floor of the indie disco. It marked the moment when the outsiders took control, no matter how briefly, of the mainstream in a way that nothing else had; not Blur and Oasis battling for number one in the charts and not even Suede at the Brits. This was their moment - by which, of course, I mean it was *my* moment.

But 'Common People' has added meaning for those of us who actually are, well, *common*.

While few of us come from the sort of homes where if you called your dad he could stop it all by writing a cheque, it is equally true that few of us could genuinely identify with the fascination of such a person with the grim realities of our lives.

For 'Common People' to mean something more than 'Britpop banger' you have to have lived the life of the common person. That doesn't mean you have to be working class to understand it or enjoy it, but it does mean that, unless you are, you can't ever 'get it'.

I didn't need to pretend I had no money growing up. Going to the dogs wasn't poverty tourism for me and my dad, it was part of our culture.

I didn't have to affect an accent and not talk proper, because I already had an accent and didn't talk proper like what the posh boys did. Second hand clothes shopping wasn't about retro fashion or shabby chic, it was financial necessity. That was my life. This was my truth. Tell me yours.

I was in the second year of my degree course when 'Common People' was released, the only person in my family ever to have made it through the gates of a university, let alone to have actually achieved a degree. Neither of my parents, none of my aunts and uncles, not a grandparent, no ancestor, not even a cousin twice removed had ever walked where I was walking. Ten years earlier my grades wouldn't have been good enough but by the mid-90s many old colleges had been granted university status and kids like me suddenly had a shot at a degree. I didn't make it to a first class place of higher learning but I had made it somewhere that nobody else in my family had. This wasn't St. Andrews or Edinburgh and many of my peers were just like me, working class first timers, grabbing their shot at something better than their parents had managed. The rest of the student body were lower middle class kids who hadn't tried hard enough at school, but even they had advantages over the likes of me. However, for the most part, these were kids like me. Common.

One weekend I travelled to Dundee to visit my girlfriend who was studying art at Duncan of Jordanstone College. As Friday night unfolded I found myself being introduced to her new friends:

a French girl here, a boy who had attended Old Glenalmond there, another girl called Verona who came from Bearsden, the bit of Glasgow that isn't all that Glasgow. All of them speaking in voices I didn't recognise, talking about things I didn't know about and dressing in ways I couldn't comprehend. There is a moment in Graham Armstrong's debut novel 'The Young Team' where the central character describes a similar night out and the awfulness of the people mocking you for, well, being you. Waving their privilege in your face, making it clear that you are not like them despite the fact that you have arrived at the same destination.

A few years ago I attended a party to celebrate the fact that my wife's old school friend had achieved something fairly impressive. It was held in a posh part of Edinburgh and at one point my wife's friend's husband approached the small group that I was part of. He had attended our wedding a few years earlier and so I said hello and held out my hand to shake his. Without blinking he looked at me and then turned his attention to someone else. Someone more important, someone more worthy of his attention and someone less common. Didn't even shake my hand. Didn't say hello. I didn't exist. This time I didn't feel awkward. I felt shame. And anger. Red hot anger. I stormed out of the venue and had to be stopped from calling a group of friends to come down and 'fix' this situation.

That's the reality of being one of the common people. No matter what you achieve, no matter how much money you earn, no matter how many qualifications you gather, you will always be reminded of your place by girls from Greece with a thirst for knowledge. That's why 'Common People' isn't the feel good hit of the summer of '95 for me, it is a reminder of who I am and where I came from.

This isn't some ridiculous [1]Class War pamphlet or the equivalent of one of those nasty little demonstrations outside of

---

1. English anarchist, famous for harassing Tory politician Jacob Rees-Mogg outside his home.

the home of some 'toff' or other. It's not the missing chapter from one of Owen Jones' books either. This isn't political. This is about the truth of how being working class can define and shape you for good and for ill and how it can twist the perception of others about you.

I'm happy that you like doing your best Jarvis on the dance floor. I like hearing everyone screaming along to the 'Wanna live with common people like YOOOOOOOUUUUUUU' bit. I love that a song like that was such a huge hit. I am thrilled to my core every time I see Pulp doing it at Glastonbury. But, and I'm sorry if you don't like this, if you don't know what it's like to be a common person then this can never mean the same thing that it means to us. You might watch 'Benefits Street' or 'The Scheme' with disbelief and find yourself laughing, but not us, we see the roaches climb the walls and we thank a God we probably don't believe in that, like Jarvis, we found a way out.

Taken from the second of their Britpop trilogy, 'Different Class' this was the moment that Jarvis Cocker became the nation's sweetheart, and he hadn't even wiggled his pert buttocks in the general direction of Michael Jackson yet.

'Different Class' is not the best Pulp album. That honour, of course, goes to 'His 'n' Hers'.

But this was, much like '(What's the Story) Morning Glory?' or 'Parklife', the album that put Pulp at the heart of the mainstream.

From the fringes to the fringes of the mainstream to the mainstream to being the mainstream.

If this had been released in 1992 it would have sold thirteen copies, with five of them being acquired by people who were linked to the band by blood. This was an album that needed Britpop and that, at the same time, defined Britpop. It is a pop record with songs of love, lust and loopy nonsense. That's the surface. Sing along anthems like 'Common People' and 'Disco

2000'. Tabloid scandals with 'Sorted for E's and Wizz'. Love songs like 'Something Changed'.

Except the anthems are not really anthems, they are hymns to the less than ordinary Ken Loach musicals, dark tales from a world that the people wailing along in their cars couldn't and didn't know existed.

Except the tabloid scandal surrounding 'Sorted for E's and Whizz' was an artificial outrage as the song is, in truth, a cautionary tale and not, as is the case with 'Trainspotting', an exercise in treating drugs as entertainment.

Except the love songs are darker than your deepest secrets.

These were not the sorts of songs that your mum and dad would have been listening to just a few years earlier, certainly not on Radio 2, and yet here we were.

The very idea that someone like Jarvis Cocker would become a national treasure, a cultural icon, a style guru and let's be honest, a legend, would have been a ridiculous notion to anyone (other than possibly Jarvis) prior to Britpop becoming a 'thing'. But that is what Jarvis became when 'Different Class' landed. He went from indie bloke to pop star in one moment.

> *'If you want to know what it is that makes Sheffield different to other cities in the UK I would say there is a very dry humour, people don't talk a great deal, people aren't so open... it takes a long time to get to know people there.'*
>
> (Jarvis Cocker, 2015)

Sheffield has a long history of producing pop groups who are ground-breaking, arty, art house, weird, wonderful and revolutionary. The new romantic soul glamour of A.B.C, the Dadaist musings of Cabaret Voltaire, the post-punk Comsat Angels, the genius of Phil Oakey and his Human League, the

47

alternative dance stylings of Moloko and their Tight Sweater - it's a list that stands up alongside the best of Manchester or Glasgow for influence, style and quality. Something in the water? Whatever it is we should be thankful.

The rain falls hard on the slate grey streets of Paisley. It must be summer. Or winter. Spring maybe. Autumn? Four seasons in one hour. I've been at the University of Paisley for about three months. I wouldn't say I was miserable - it was actually far worse than that. I had been low in high school but I was sinking to new depths here. I hadn't managed to secure a place in halls so the hedonistic life I had imagined wasn't happening. Instead I had secured an attic bedroom in the home of an elderly couple which basically cast me as a flower in the attic. Their home was miles away from the city centre and so most of my evenings were spent hunched over my record player and dreaming of a life less ordinary.

Bill Clinton was in the White House. John Major was in Number 10. It's possible that Mr Blobby was at number one in the charts. It was a Monday. On my way home from some lecture or other I stopped off at Stereo One behind Paisley Gilmour Street train station. It was a big record store and I have a feeling there was an upstairs and everything. I didn't smoke or drink (I still don't) so despite my meagre budget I had more money than most of my contemporaries for the things that really mattered like clothes, copies of the NME and records. As I browsed the racks a sleeve jumped out at me. I didn't know if it was a band called 'Lipgloss' who had released a single called 'Pulp' or a band called 'Pulp' who had released a single called 'Lipgloss'. I hadn't heard of either one. I stood looking at the cover for a while. It made me feel a bit wobbly in my stomach. Was that tall, firm, hard lipstick meant to look like…? Nah. Nope. No way. But then I looked at those ruby red lips, shaped for sin, parted - were they meant to be suggesting…? Nah. Nope. No way.

I bought it. I trudged back to the attic. I listened to it. It wasn't a song about sex, which is what I had assumed because of the cover. It was a harrowing tale of a relationship turned sour. A relationship blighted by machismo. A relationship built on the abuse of power.

A woman broken, battered and bruised by a man who doesn't love her, who never loved her and who doesn't care about her? It left me reeling.

It made me want to dance and sing along. It made me want to find the girl, fling my arms around her and let her know that things could get better, that there were good people in this ugly world too and then prove it to her.

It was the sort of thing Morrissey used to write. The voice was pure Northern soul. I'll be honest with you, I was smitten.

Jarvis Branson Cocker was born in Sheffield in 1963. Fifteen years later he was already set on the path to pop stardom when, alongside his school friend Peter Dalton, they formed a band called 'Arabicus Pulp'. Initially Cocker had wanted to call the band 'Pulp' after the 1972 Michael Caine film of the same name but Dalton felt that this was too short and so they added a twisted version of a coffee bean found in the pages of the Financial Times (Arabicas) and they were ready to go. Between 1978 and 1992 there were Peel sessions, flirtations with various styles, line-up changes and riots.

There was no overnight success for Jarvis but instead the sort of long, fraught, tiring, march towards the top of the pops *and* Top of the Pops that would make a wonderful rags to riches Hollywood tale. One cannot help but feel that this was the right way for him though, that he had to really *wait* for his time to finally come for it to be as glorious as it turned out to be.

When I picked up my copy of 'Lipgloss' from Stereo One, the line-up of the band was Jarvis on vocals, Candida Doyle on keyboards, Russell Senior on guitar/violin (of *course* they had a violin player), Mark Webber on guitar/keyboards, Steve Mackey on bass and Nick Banks on drums. It was this group that would propel Pulp, and Jarvis, from the fringes of the fringes of the mainstream to the sort of success that normally eludes eccentric boys from Sheffield and their mates and turned them into a cultural phenomenon.

> *'Pulp was a way of looking at the world and ordinary people.'*
>
> (Jarvis Cocker)

She was a girl. I was a boy. She wasn't, as it turned out, *the* girl. I most certainly wasn't *the* boy.

My father's 'birds and the bees' chat consisted of him explaining that a fishing rod comes in two sections and that if you popped this section into this section then you got a complete fishing rod. I can remember being with him as far as there being two sections and that those two sections could join together but he lost me when he returned to the fishing rod analogy. That conversation made the first time very awkward - I doubt it was her first time and I think she was genuinely shocked to see me approaching in waders and clutching a Shakespeare ugly stick. It's all fine now though. I'm married, so I don't have sex.

By the time Pulp released 'Do You Remember the First Time?' they had featured in *that* famous issue of Select magazine alongside Suede, Denim and The Auteurs, as part of the front line troops in the Britpop battle against grunge. However, although that issue of Select made it look like Britpop was going to amount to nothing more than a gaggle of slightly effeminate young men in charity second hand clothes casting envious glances back towards Bowie and T-Rex, with the benefit of hindsight, we now know that the scene became something very different to that, something 'traditional'.

'Do You Remember the First Time?' didn't just arrive as a single but as a short film too where the likes of Alison Steadman, Terry Hall, Bob Mortimer and Justine Frischmann discussed, described and dissected their first times. It highlighted the fact that both Pulp and Jarvis (as a separate entity) were more than a pop group. They had loftier aspirations. Art. Film. Moving Image. Poetry. Cultural commentary.

> *'That thing where two people start wearing matching clothes, their personalities start to merge, they know exactly what each other's thinking, and they haven't a whole personality of their own any more, they've just got half of something else. And if that's taken away, they're less than a person.'*
>
> (Jarvis Cocker, 1995)

'His 'n' Hers' is a collection of eleven songs that deal with the truth, the reality, the horror, the dread, the fear and the dreadful boredom that the conventional world trades in. By adding in hints of the unconventional and tossing in the sort of dry, uniquely Northern humour that often defines bands from that part of the UK, the ordinary becomes extraordinary at the nib of Cocker's pen.

'Joyriders' tells the humdrum tale of a group of boys who live for the thrill of driving their cars as fast as they can on a Saturday night. They're not nice boys. They have a sneering contempt for the bloke in the Jesus sandals. They pick up a girl and take her to the reservoir and something awful happens. Another girl in a hideous relationship fills the lines of 'Pink Glove' he doesn't love her, he just wants her to dress up for him in something tight. Something pink. But if that's all that relationship is then who is she? The whole album is littered with these stories and with a musical and lyrical prowess that takes your breath away.

'His 'n' Hers' put Pulp on the front pages of the music papers and, thanks in large part, to the joy of Jarvis they stayed there for a very long time. The final single taken from the album was an EP. entitled 'Sisters' and it featured four tracks but as far as the record buying public were concerned it featured only one - 'Babies'. It reached number nineteen in the charts and now twenty four years later it still fills the dance floor at any indie night or Britpop celebration with boys and girls doing their very best imitation of Jarvis. Like a floor filled with stick insects being delivered a mild electric shock.

By the time that 'This is Hardcore' dropped onto shelves in March 1998, Britpop was already a distant memory. We had left behind the eccentricities and excitement of Denim, Suede, Elastica, Blur and even Pulp themselves and replaced them with one Oasis covers band after another. Rock was running the world of British pop. All the hope that songs like 'Do You Remember the First Time?' had offered to young people like me had been extinguished and our moment was over.

I'm not a party person. I don't understand why you would want to go somewhere where there isn't Haribo, Netflix and your own record collection and where there are people you don't know and whose confidence, drunken joviality, popularity and good looks will serve only to highlight your own shyness, misery, awkwardness and ugly mug when you could stay at home where there IS Haribo, Netflix and your own records and where the only other people are the ones whom you have carefully selected because of their ability to tolerate your myriad defects. I've never understood it. Ever.

The only party I've ever enjoyed was Britpop and that was mainly because I was able to enjoy it from the privacy of my own bedroom or in the equally private confines of a gig where I was just another face in the crowd.

Perfect.

By the time we had all discovered that actually things couldn't only get better and that the new dawn promised by New Labour was probably just more of the same but with a minimum wage, it was 1998 and the Britpop party had moved past the stage where the last drunken stragglers were boarding the night bus home and had instead reached the stage where you are heaving a comatose stranger into the back of a cab while simultaneously trying not to think about the exact nature of the stain in the middle of your sitting room carpet.

It wasn't pretty.

No record better captures the post-Britpop fug better than 'This is Hardcore'. It starts, as every new day does, with 'The Fear'. The only magic in evidence here is of the very darkest sort as Cocker seems to be giving voice to the thoughts that surface most frequently as I lie in bed, drive in the car, walk to the shops and, well, you get the idea.

Loneliness turned up to ten, no matter how many people I'm with. Losing the plot, even though I'm smiling. Making out I'm OK, when I promise you that I'm not. I can't even define what it is that I'm frightened of. Searching for some kind of life, not just an existence.

'The Fear' gives me the fear but it also makes me feel less afraid and like someone else obviously feels this way too. The company, and comfort, of strangers.

Fame, from the outside, looks like the most wonderful thing. Everything glitters. There's gold against your soul twenty four hours a day. Glamour. Glitz. Adoration. Love? It's all yours for the taking. No, you're not taking, you're accepting because it's all being flung at you.

The truth is, I think, very different. I've been close to one or two people who were on the subs bench for the Z list starting eleven of celebrity and even that level of not quite fame has a very unsettling effect on people. They were never really able to return to being themselves because they were 'on' all of the time. They also suffered from never being told anything honest because hangers on, industry people, fans simply threw relentless praise at them and accepted any unacceptable behaviour from them. That, I think, is unhealthy.

There was a religious fervour attached to a lot of the main players in Britpop: Damon Albarn and his angelic face, Liam Gallagher as the saviour of rock and roll and Jarvis himself as Christ in the temple chasing out the money lenders when he rushed the stage at the Brits during Michael Jackson's own Jesus act - if you listen to the audio of that event carefully you can actually hear Jarvis saying 'In my father's house?' as he wiggles his bottom.

'Party Hard' is a song that's been dipped in so much sleaze that it could be a guest on Jeremy Kyle. It's the dark side of fame writ large. When Jarvis states within the first line that he wants to be liked by everyone, you know that this is a song about the difference between the public perception of fame and the bitter reality of it. There's meaningless sex with men like Bill Clinton staining the garments of women, there's the relentless demands of the public and the shallow nature of showbiz friendships. There is no need to have experienced fame to be able to relate to any of this of course because bad sex, people making unreasonable demands of you and hollow half-friendships are common currency for anyone who has a heart. That's the genius of Cocker - making the extraordinary, ordinary and the ordinary extraordinary.

By the time 'This is Hardcore' was released we were all a little older - in my case I was just about to turn twenty five which now seems very young but which, at the time, seemed so very old. A quarter of a century. I was older than my dad had been when he became a parent. I was soon to be married. I had finished my degree. I had a full time job. I wasn't in a band any more. I was a grown up. It was awful. All of it.

Jarvis was a decade older. At thirty five he was, really, a middle-aged man. He had spent the last five years at parties, taking drugs, being adored, prancing and dancing, wiggling his bottom and baring his soul to millions of strangers. It's not a normal existence. He had partied hard and now, one couldn't help but feel, he was questioning whether it had really been worth it.

That idea of time wasted, of the link between the highs of fame and the realities of normality runs through 'Help the Aged'. Its title may play like a novelty record but, once again, there are grand themes and big questions lurking at its heart. The very idea that old age, or indeed any age other than the one we were, was looming seemed impossible. The passing of time and all of its terrible crimes is a painful thing to experience as all of our boundless energy, relentless positivity, carefree abandon and full head of hair is replaced by tiredness, cynicism, worry and male pattern baldness. Just me?

Title track 'This is Hardcore' is as sleazy and sordid musically and lyrically as the title suggests and is a rumination on the transactional nature of sex in the nineties. It's a lust song about love replaced by the dull ache of desire for desire's sake. I think that it's also a song with something to say about the burgeoning 'I just wanna be famous' culture that was beginning to hold the nation's youth in its vice like grip as Fame Academy, Pop Stars, X-Factor, Britain's Got Talent et al have made fame for fame's sake seem like a career option. The idea of being good, producing art, having something to say, leaving your mark, inspiring others were all replaced by a Christmas number one and a few years of switching on the Christmas lights in your hometown.

'T.V Movie' though is a very different beast, it's a bona fide hymn to love faded and passed away. Full of yearning and desire with a pulse, it's the song we would all like to have written to the first girl/boy we ever loved and who only loved us back for long enough to just make us love them even more. Missing someone the way that

Jarvis describes in this song is the thing that makes love, real love, so special and worth fighting for. It's a perfect companion piece to 'A Little Soul' which follows it, which is another love song, this time about love that has been lost, misplaced or discarded by someone who didn't know quite what they had until it was gone. Cocker is a people watcher, a non-participant observer, at least until he participates. He looks and he listens and that's why his songs seem so honest and so familiar to we common people.

In 'I'm a Man', Cocker wonders what the point of being a 'man' is if all it amounts to is fags, booze, cars and, well, not much else really. He seems disappointed, disconnected and disturbed by these tired tropes of masculinity. If life is made up of those things then I'm not sure there is a satisfactory answer. Morrissey asks the same questions in 'I'm Not a Man' from 'World Peace is None of Your Business' just fifteen years after Jarvis.

The character at the heart of 'Seductive Barry' agrees with George Michael's position that sex is both natural and good, he loves a bit of the other and he's very keen to let you in on every intimate detail of the love scene he's about to act out. That love scene appears to either feature some lucky chap who has landed a night of passion with the object of his desires or alternatively it's about some poor bloke who is pleasuring himself while looking at a poster of a scantily clad lay-dee. You decide.

'Sylvia' would have been perfectly at home with some of the folks who inhabited the songs on 'His 'n' Hers' some four years earlier. A girl who is settling for the wrong boys, the wrong town, the wrong everything. It's a sad song. An all too familiar tale. Young women who have had their dreams quashed, their wants and needs pushed into the background and their hopes and desires relegated by small town minds, old fashioned attitudes and goodness knows what else. But Jarvis won't have it. 'Keep believin'' he implores her from the sidelines. Let's all pray for Sylvia.

A fanfare for the common man arrives with 'Glory Days'. Unfulfilled potential and wasted days are writ large on the faces of the kids in the song. Hanging out in cafes, genius unrealised due to apathy, astronauts in the making who clean toilets instead - they could do anything, if only they could be bothered. Despite a jaunty tune driving things along it is, at its heart, another achingly sad song. I reckon I'm one of those kids now, someone who made the wrong choices at the wrong time, indulged an inability and unwillingness to stretch myself and has now found that my astronaut days are behind me. Tragic innit.

'The meek shall inherit absolutely nothing at all' is the line that sums up the end of the Britpop era and the end of the party better than any other. 'The Day After the Revolution' may, or may not, be a nod to the New Labour election victory of 1997. What seemed like a genuinely revolutionary moment in British history with the end of eighteen years of a deeply unpopular government, the promise of Blair, Cool Britannia, Noel in Number 10, was already beginning to seem like another false dawn. Of course none of us knew quite how far away from the promise of those days the New Labour project would drift but the idea that things could only get better was already seeming unlikely.

It's very possible that 'This is Hardcore' is the full stop to the Britpop story. While other albums came and new bands emerged it's hard not to look back now and see that the greatest moment in British pop and pop culture history was over as soon as the needle lifted at the end of this album.

Chapter 5

Waking Up

Elastica

I can't be sure.

I can't be precise.

I reckon it's November 1993.

It is certainly 1993.

I'm sure of that.

The November bit is guess work.

I want to say I am standing inside the Sub Club on Jamaica Street, Glasgow. That seems like the sort of place I would have been in November 1993.

I should have kept a diary.

Here is what I know for sure - sitting at the bar is Justine Frischmann.

I know it is her because I have seen her face in the NME and the Melody Maker and Select and Vox and in every other magazine that has even a passing connection with pop music. She's everywhere. You cannot avoid her. You wouldn't want to. She is the sort of person that attracts your attention. She is articulate, clever, funny and achingly cool. Hip without the hipster.

A few days ago her band Elastica had released their debut single 'Stutter' and now they are on a tour of the UK with Kingmaker. Most people inside the Sub Club are here to see Kingmaker. I have little interest in Kingmaker. I am here, with my best friend Chris, to see Elastica. We are, for the first time in our miserable little lives, ahead of the game - we have seen the future and it is star shaped.

'Stutter' is a crucial moment in the history and evolution of Britpop. It is a landmark. It arrives at roughly the same time as the 'Bellyache' EP from Echobelly, the 'Alice' EP from Sleeper and 'Kent' and 'Diminished Clothes', the first two releases from Salad. The patronisingly named 'female fronted bands' sub-scene had arrived. Sisters were doing it for themselves.

With a lyric that dealt with the *'occasional problem of drunken male impotence'* this was clearly and defiantly, a song that wasn't going to play by the rules. No faux feminism of the type being hawked by the Spice Girls and their call for young women everywhere to dress up like every male fantasy ever peddled by marketing departments at record labels ever and there was no 'zig-ah-zig-ah' either. Instead here was a woman in control. A woman with things to say and who was going to say them no matter how uncomfortable they may make certain people feel.

Funny.

Honest.

Shocking.

Sexual and sexy.

Dig the new breed.

While enrolled at the Bartlett architecture school at ULU in the late 1980s, Justine Frischmann met a boy called Brett[1]. He wanted to start a band. She thought that was an excellent idea and so, together with some other boys, that is exactly what they did. They played a few gigs, wrote a few songs and then played a few more gigs but it did not seem like it was going anywhere. Justine and Brett were in love. That made things a bit more complicated. Especially when Justine left the band and also Brett.

---

1. Brett Anderson, lead singer of Suede. Justine's impact on his development as an artist and her crucial role in the Suede story are told brilliantly and intimately in Anderson's memoirs 'Coal Black Mornings' and 'Afternoons With the Blinds Drawn'.

Striking out on her own Justine began to assemble a group who could bring to life her own pop visions. Along with another former member of Suede, Justin Welch[2], Frischmann brought in Annie Holland and Donna Matthews to form Elastica. Taking their musical inspirations from punk and post-punk they managed to create music that was spiky, angular, angry, fast, funny and deliciously catchy.

For a short while they played under the name 'Onk' which, I am sure we can all agree, is a magnificent name for anything or anyone but which would, in all likelihood, not have captured the attention of the press, or the public, in quite the same way as 'Elastica'.

They were soon signed to Deceptive, which was run by Steve Lamacq[3], and it was on that label that 'Stutter' was released. At this point the Elastica story couldn't get any Britpoppier if it tried. A direct link to Suede, Damon Albarn[4] lurking in the shadows, Steve Lamacq whose Evening Session was the home of Britpop on the air, and songs that were influenced by Wire, the Buzzcocks, Bowie and other glam, punk and post-punk nobility.

It could have been dreadful.

If the songs were no good then the whole thing would have been the perfect embodiment of all the half-truths that critics of the era like to use to ridicule it. All surface but no feeling.

It wasn't dreadful though, it was great.

I sidle up to Justine Frischmann in the half-empty Sub Club.

Nobody has a mobile phone and only the anorakiest of the anorak brigade bring cameras to concerts.

There can be no selfie. Also nobody knew what the hell a selfie was in 1993.

---

2. Welch was replaced in Suede by Simon Gilbert.
3. Radio 1 DJ, host of the Evening Session along with Jo Wiley.
4. Frischmann was dating Albarn for much of the early part of the Britpop story; they were a sort of indie Posh and Becks.

'Um, you're Justine from Elastica aren't you?' I manage to squeak.

I've got no idea where this is going.

I don't have any end game.

I'm not trying to chat her up as after all, she is dating the prettiest boy on the pop block right now.

I've seen a famous person and I've plunged headlong into an encounter with no thought about my emotional safety.

'Yes,' replies Justine.

'...............' a dreadful, heavy, almost physical silence fills the space between us, which seems to be growing wider with every passing second.

'Are you looking forward to the gig?' says the pop star, exhibiting kindness and pity to an extent that I really don't deserve.

'Yeah. Thanks,' is all I can muster.

Then, for reasons that I don't understand now and that I certainly didn't understand then, I leaned in and kissed her on the cheek. She doesn't look horrified, she looks sad for me. A sort of romantic pity fills her eyes and I stumble away.

I don't know.

I don't know.

I was very young.

I was a bit star struck.

Maybe I thought it was a very 'London' thing to do?

When I return to my friend he looks at me with a mixture of horror, repulsion, and contempt.

'What the fuck was that?' he asks.

'Shut up Chris.'

'There's something wrong with you,' he says.

I don't reply.

He is right.

There is something wrong with me.

At the start of 1994, Elastica released their second single, 'Line Up' and it immediately confirmed the fact that they were a band deserving of your love. It is a brilliant little sliver of pop. A lot of people agreed because it reached number twenty in the charts.

It is a bouncy, buoyant, bubbly, blast and blitz of art-school bop that saw kids rushing for the dance floor at indie nights up and down the country whenever they heard Justine start to make those puking noises.

The real joy of 'Line Up' though was not to be found in the three minutes and fifteen seconds of the single itself but was instead lurking on the b-side. There be pop monsters. Eighty seconds of punky, spunky, chunky naughtiness that would make Russell Brand blush.

'Vaseline' was not a hymn to the moisture insulation properties of this petroleum based lubricant. It was a filthy little song about those bedroom activities that may, on occasion, require a little extra *goo*.

Rude.

'Connection' followed as a single later in the year and, like 'Line Up', it was a massive hit free from any controversy whatsoever.

Let's move on.

Sorry...what?

Three girl what?

Rhumba?

What's that?

A song.

By who? [5]

Hold on, I'll go and give it a listen.

Back in a sec.

Ah.

It does sound quite similar.

---

5. 'Connection' bore an uncanny similarity to the 1977 song by Wire, 'Three Girl Rhumba'. A similarity that resulted in an out of court settlement and a re-writing of the credits for the song.

Fine.

It's exactly the same.

'Talent borrows, genius steals.'[6]

Clever old Elastica.

As Elastica leave the stage of the Sub Club I am dizzy.

They have played a set that would have lasted for three hours for someone like Bruce Springsteen and condensed it into about thirty-three minutes. It felt like they played dozens of songs or maybe more. Maybe they played every song ever. They just played them all really quickly. It was a riot of spiky pop glory, like the entire Stock Aitken and Waterman back catalogue being played by a gang of hedgehogs dressed in black.

Justin had bludgeoned his drum kit into submission.

Donna had set the room and possibly the wider environs of Greater Glasgow on fire with her ferocious melody making.

Annie had threatened to put out that fire with her icy cool shenanigans on bass.

Justine had been... a *star*. Glamorous in DM boots, faded black denim jeans and a black t-shirt. A Hollywood starlet for the indie boys and girls of the nascent Britpop scene.

I fell in love with every single one of them.

'Waking Up' arrived in February 1995 and was an even bigger hit than those that had come before. It reached number thirteen in the UK charts and was free from any controversy whatsoever.

Let's move on.

Sorry...what?

No more what?

Heroes? [7]

---

6. Oscar Wilde, he said everything didn't he?

7. 'Waking Up' resulted in a lawsuit from The Stranglers who argued that the song bore an uncanny similarity to their 1977 single 'No More Heroes'. The case was settled out of court.

What's that?

A song.

By The Stranglers?

Hold on, I'll go and give it a listen.

Back in a sec.

Ah.

It does sound quite similar.

Fine.

It's exactly the same.

'Talent borrows, genius steals.'

Clever old Elastica.

Again!

The much anticipated debut album 'Elastica' arrived the following month and hit the number one spot in the UK album chart. By the end of the year it had sold over one million copies. It also managed to make its way to number sixty six on the Billboard chart in the USA.

Frankly, it was massive.

It kicked off with 'Line Up' and its sneering, near contemptuous attack on the things and people in the music industry that made Justine feel ill. It's the perfect way to start a pop album. Then it was the seventy three second eponymous hymn to Annie, which is the sort of song that makes you feel glad to be alive with guitars that are strummed so vigorously that you fear for the instrument and the player, while drums are beaten, a bass throbs and Justine does *Justine*.

'Connection' was followed by 'Car Song' which was a song about the joys of motorway driving. The views, the tarmac, the service stations, the jams - although I have heard people suggest that the whole thing is a smutty little song about making the beast with two backs in the confines of a Ford Fiesta. I find that very hard to believe. Whatever the true meaning of the song, it deserves its place in your top ten for the line 'Sometimes I just can't function, my heart's spaghetti junction.' Brilliant.

'Smile' is one hundred seconds long. It starts with a Ramones-y '1-2-3-4'. Justine sounds like the cool kid at school that you really wanted to be mates with but who had already figured out that you, and everyone else in a fifty mile radius, were losers who weren't worthy of their time. Just me? Fine.

The definition of cool is difficult to get agreement on. Everyone has their own thoughts on the issue of who, or what, is or isn't 'cool'. For many years there was no definitive answer to what the gold standard for 'cool' was - mainly because there was nothing to measure things against. Then Elastica wrote 'Hold Me Now' and Justine Frischmann delivered the coolest vocal in the history of rock and roll. Bored, snooty, arrogant, obnoxious - it was thrilling. She could have been singing 'Fix You' by Coldplay and it would have sounded cool - that's how cool she was on that song.

'S.O.F.T' and 'Indian Song' were two very different beasts. When I saw Elastica for a second time at King Tut's Wah Wah Hut in Glasgow it was 'S.O.F.T' that had the biggest impact. It was sexy in a way that the Kings of Leon had wanted to be with the turgid 'Sex On Fire' (or whatever the hell that song was called, I'm not looking for it on Bing). It had a sleazy, slinky, sassy vibe and I can vividly remember my stomach flipping as I stood in the crowd that night. 'Indian Song' sounds like the sort of thing Suede would have recorded had Justine hung around, and that's a good thing.

The next two songs 'Blue' and 'All-Nighter' had a combined running time of three minutes and fifty four seconds. Too many bands forget the joy of this sort of smash and grab pop gubbins. Melody. Riff. Some words. Biff. Bang. Pow. Ace. The same trick is repeated after 'Waking Up' with '2:1' and 'Vaseline' coming in at exactly the same run time, although that might not be true, I can't do sums, but even if it is not true, it *feels* true. That's what matters.

Before we return to the very beginning of the story with 'Stutter' at the album's conclusion, we are treated to a 'proper' song in the shape of 'Never Here' and I'm sorry to labour the point and to get hung up on this but, really, the only word is *cool*. It has a great melody, a catchy chorus and another icy, too-cool-for-school vocal from Justine.

That was it.

Fifteen songs in about the same number of minutes.

It's an album that rarely features in discussions about the best of the era, mainly because people like me get hung up on 'His 'n' Hers', 'Definitely Maybe', 'Modern Life is Rubbish', 'Dog Man Star' and the other big hitters, which is terribly unfair as 'Elastica' stands shoulder to shoulder with any of those records and suggested that a brilliant career was about to be launched...

It is 1996.

I'm with Chris again.

We are standing at the back entrance of the Rothes Halls in Glenrothes.

Glenrothes is a dump.

It is the dictionary definition of nowhere.

Elastica are playing a gig in aid of 'Zero Tolerance', a charity who offer support to victims of domestic violence.

Chris and I don't have tickets.

We can't afford them.

Our plan is to wait until someone from the band ventures out of the venue and to accost them, which will be our first attempt at blagging.

Look, here comes someone.

For a moment we can't speak.

Shortly after the release of 'Elastica', Annie had jumped ship and had been replaced by someone called Sheila [8] and here she was 'round the back of the Rothes Halls.

---

8. Sheila Chipperfield joined the band in 1996. She was then replaced by the returning Annie Holland in 1998.

'Sheila! Any chance you could get us in tonight?'

This isn't exactly subtle but it is, undoubtedly, direct.

'Yeah. What are your names?'

A second album wouldn't arrive until 2000. It was called 'The Menace' and, if we have to be honest, it lacked the lustre of the debut. The journey to 'The Menace' had seen both Donna and Annie leave permanently. Justine had split from Damon. Her flatmate, Loz from Kingmaker, contributed to a couple of Eno-esque tracks. The Fall loomed large in the mix, which is fine if you like The Fall and hate songs with actual tunes.

It was a guddle.

A mess.

A last gasp.

It should have been *brilliant*.

'The Menace' reached number twenty four on release and received favourable if not exactly gushing reviews. Andrew Collins in Q called it 'surprisingly good'. Damning with faint praise? Sort of. The surprise wasn't that the album was good, the surprise was that anyone should have been surprised. Frischmann and Matthews had already proven that they had the ability to write great pop songs. Maybe there was another surprise in the story at this point and that was that the album had arrived at all. Heroin had become the drug of choice for lots of people in the Britpop story, including some people very close to Elastica. It certainly had come to play a part in the life of Matthews. Few people under the influence of heroin can be said to be 'go getters'. Then there was the fact that Frischmann had broken up with Damon Albarn during their hiatus. Drugs, broken hearts and, after aborted attempts to record in 1996, the departure of both Matthews and Annie Holland. None of this is the sort of soil from which one would expect great art to blossom.

My own response to the album on its release was one of contempt. I listened to the opening track 'Mad Dog God Dam' and decided it was a bloody racket and didn't bother listening to the rest of it for a very long time. It was too angular, too spiky, too peculiar. The constant barrage of blokes with guitars and bad haircuts in the years since the end of Britpop had laid waste to my ability to really listen to music. I had become a dreadful bore, a one-dimensional consumer, a dullard. At that point it was impossible for a record like 'The Menace' to have had any impact on me. Fortunately I was able to move on, free myself from the shackles of bucket hats and Ben Sherman. Praise be.

Otherwise I would still only be listening to music from twenty-five years ago while trapped in a cultural and musical ghetto.

White bread.

Plain white bread.

When I listened to 'The Menace' properly for the first time I was struck by one moment in particular. 'My Sex' is an Eno-esque mess, mass and mash of electronic noises, spoken word and beautiful synths that left me reeling. A hymn to love. 'To walk through the wardrobe of other bodies we have known' might just be the most beautiful line in a song ever. Yet it's not even the most beautiful line in the song. That honour goes to 'What I want is to love you everywhere and everyhow'. It might not even be that those lines are especially beautiful but to hear Frischmann deliver them in a near whisper and with absolute conviction is enough to break your heart. It stands, or lies, as a tender counterpoint to the more brutal delights of 'Love Like Ours' with lines like: 'A love like ours will never die, break my bonds, break my back' being the closest it gets to the delicate delights of 'My Sex'. It is one of the closest tracks on the album to the songs that so delighted the fans five years earlier.

There are more tracks that recall the wonky, post-punk, punk-pop, spills of the debut album too like 'Your Arse My Place' and 'Generator', which can only be listened to when one is wearing Doctor Martens, black jeans and a leather jacket - a floppy fringe is optional. They sound like 'Elastica' and that is a good thing. But it isn't good enough. Not if you want more from the bands you love than simple repetition. Fortunately, Frischmann understood how important it was not to stand still and so the album also includes one of the most creative, distinctive and disruptive voices in British music history - Mark E. Smith. Smith was involved in the writing and recording of both 'How He Wrote Elastica Man' (a playful nod to The Fall's 'How I Wrote Elastic Man') and 'KB'. Smith's presence ensures that, just as with his own band, the music is urgent, forceful and experimental.

'The Menace' does have a problem but it isn't the album - it is the presence of its predecessor, 'Elastica'. The success of that album, the love that people have for it and its part in the Britpop story, all combined to create a curious weight that was, almost inevitably, going to crush anything that followed it. It would have been interesting if 'The Menace' had arrived first, but this isn't an episode of 'Quantum Leap' and so we have to play with the hand we have been dealt by history.

I could do that really annoying thing that people do where they claim to prefer one of a band's less popular albums rather than the one that everyone else loves in order to get some likes on Twitter, or to provoke a reaction from you as you read this, but I'm not that guy. Not now. 'The Menace' is a good record and I would even go so far as to say that at times and in certain places it is a *great* album, and it definitely deserves more than the slightly sniffy reception it normally receives. What matters is not the end but the fact that Elastica succeeded in releasing one of the best albums of the nineties, unleashed a clutch of dementedly brilliant singles, pushed the idea of women in indie rock forward and generally showed how much could be achieved just by being cool and more talented than any of your male peers.

Chapter 6

Rock 'n' Roll Stars

Oasis

When Peggy Sweeney first married Tommy Gallagher it wouldn't have entered into her head that she was entering a world of mayhem, abuse and violence. Like lots of other young Irish Catholic girls she would have taken her marriage vows seriously and would have been set upon being a good wife and mother but sadly for Peggy, Tommy Gallagher didn't seem to place as much importance in the love and honour parts of his vows. Setting up home in Manchester in the 1960s like so many other Irish families, things would prove to be hard economically as well as emotionally for her but when her three boys arrived she set about providing them with the love and support that she had rarely found within her marriage.

Paul the eldest, Noel the middle brother and Liam, the baby of the bunch, found home to be a place filled with love and discipline from their mother and bullying and violence from their father, with Noel suffering most directly from the ugly side of his father - with the result that like many young people who are victims of domestic violence he developed a stammer which took four years of speech therapy to eradicate. None of the brothers have ever spoken in detail about their experiences at home but a look at their characters, their relationships with one another (particularly Noel and Liam) and their rare public comments reveals that their childhood was a dark place.

'I don't look back on that time with any regret or sadness, it kind of makes you who you are.'
(Noel Gallagher, RTE 'The Meaning of Life')

Manchester has a long history of Irish immigrants settling in the city. By 1841 nearly one in ten people in the city were Irish. Many of them lived in a slum area of Ancoats called 'Little Ireland', an area of the city that Engels labelled *'the most disgusting spot of all'* in his *Condition of the Working Class in England'*. Poverty marked the lives of many of those early immigrants and indeed it would continue to do so for many of those who followed them over the decades. Even now the links between Ireland and Manchester are strong and the annual Manchester Irish Festival is the largest in the UK and one of the largest in the world, while the terraces of both of Manchester's football clubs also have pockets of Irish supporters making up the numbers.

Right across the UK, those Irish immigrants have made their mark on the music scene. John Lydon, Kevin Rowland, Morrissey, Johnny Marr (Maher) and, of course, the Gallagher brothers are just some of the musicians and songwriters who have defined, shaped and forever altered the world of popular music in the UK and beyond. It's impossible to imagine what the music scene in the UK would sound like without the musicality of those Irish immigrant homes.

The combination of a working class, Irish immigrant, poverty marked childhood and the dark presence of a violent father is one which would have broken many young men. The scars of domestic violence are not just left on the bodies of their victims but deep in the minds of the witnesses. A different path is forged from this background for others though, with a strength of character, a drive to escape, a desire to rise above and a hunger to be better than their circumstances have dictated which leads them to become something, *someone*.

When Paul 'Guigsy' McGuigan invited Liam Gallagher to join his band 'Rain' he was probably motivated as much by the fact that in Liam they would have a criminally good looking and achingly cool front man than by any belief in the youngest Gallagher's ability to sing or write songs. The band also featured Paul Arthurs, who was also known as Bonehead, on guitar and this would be the beginning of his songwriting partnership with Liam. The band rehearsed, they wrote some songs and they played a handful of gigs. It is safe to say that Rain did not exactly set the Manchester scene of the early 90s ablaze with their offerings. The only buzz was from their speakers.

Noel Gallagher, on the other hand, had enjoyed more success with his first foray into the music business as a roadie for Madchester icons the Inspiral Carpets. Thanks to this gig Noel was able to leave Manchester and see a bit of the world and what it had to offer. It also offered him a front row seat at the theatre of the absurd that is life on the road - and he liked what he saw. There was also a lot of down-time, which meant that there was room to practice his guitar playing and to work on the songs that filled his head. Like lots of people though he couldn't work out how to actually do the things he was watching other people do every night.

At some point in 1991, Noel caught his little brother's band playing live. 'Just awful' is how Noel has described what he saw and heard. Liam doesn't disagree, describing Rain as being 'shit'. What Noel *did* see though was an actual *band*. They didn't have any actual songs but they could play and in Liam they had a touch of star quality - someone who could lift them from being another band to being *the* band. A name change was suggested and a few of his own songs were played to the others and that was that - the world might not have been listening to the two brothers apart but now that they were together, there wasn't going to be any way to ignore them.

The story of what happened next is a part of rock and roll history. The drive to Glasgow from Manchester. The Creation showcase at King Tuts Wah Wah Hut. Alan McGee in the crowd. A record deal. Simple.

What is interesting about this story is not the balls of these Mancunian chancers simply hitting the road convinced of their own brilliance and the rewards that just had to be theirs but is, in fact, the rather unusual presence of McGee. Any other label boss may well have arrived in time for the headline act that night, if indeed they had any interest in seeing any live music at all in a tiny venue with no VIP section, and then may well have decided to ask some other less important A&R man to take a second look at an unknown band whose name he couldn't remember.

Not Alan McGee.

Alan McGee is as much of a genius as any of the acts he has pushed, managed, promoted and evangelised about. His genius isn't in writing or singing though. His genius lies in his ability to have remained forever the kid from East Kilbride who formed a punk band and then never lost the feeling he got when he first heard those formative records that have inspired him for nearly forty years. He's a Peter Pan figure. The boy who has refused to grow up and start listening to Mumford & Sons. He has been a passionate, blistering and boisterous face and voice on the fringes of the mainstream since his adolescence and even when he made it big he never lost his passion or his recklessness.

McGee was convinced that he had witnessed the greatest band he had ever seen that night on the stage of King Tuts[1]. Something inside him said that this was it. This was going to be the band that would change everything and he knew that he couldn't let them get away. A deal was offered and accepted and

---

1. King Tuts Wah Wah Hut in Glasgow is a legendary live music venue.

a match was made in Heaven. It was a decision that was going to change the lives of everyone in the band and of many people who heard them. It was also going to change British popular culture and the nature of Britpop, although not necessarily for the better.

1994 saw the release of 'Supersonic', the band's first single. It arrived in the form of four minutes and forty three seconds of nonsensical lyrics about a girl called Elsa accompanied by lazy, hazy drums, a bass line that drifted into your bones and a melody so steeped in British rock history that it could have been by any band from any time but still sounded like nothing else. Crucially it also featured a vocal that couldn't have been provided by any other singer ever - here was a voice that demanded you listen, *really* listen and then when you finished, demanded that you go back and listen again.

This isn't hindsight talking. On its release everybody knew that this was something great. Keith Cameron in the NME summed up the mood of the nation:

> *'If Oasis didn't exist, it's hard to believe anyone would have the gall to invent them. Great bands out of Manchester there has been, even ones that harked back to previous great Manchester bands, but nothing like this...Thrilling? Absolutely. Stars? Inevitably. And? Simply a great rock 'n' roll group.'*[2]

What followed was something even more incredible, something even more impressive, something even more inspiring. An album of such importance that it is now talked about in the same reverential tones as the debut Stone Roses album, 'The Queen is Dead' by The Smiths or 'Never Mind the Bollocks'

---

2. New Musical Express, 9 April 1994

by the Sex Pistols. An album that has sold over fifteen million copies worldwide, that has gone platinum seven times in the UK, that was the fastest selling debut of all time up to that point and that topped the charts in more countries than you could name (even with the help of an atlas). It is the defining album of its time.

'Definitely Maybe' is the album that announced to the world that things were about to change. There were new kids on the block and they were here to ensure that there wouldn't ever be any need for a band like New Kids on the Block ever again. It was an album that was inspired by everyone from the Sex Pistols to The Smiths, the Stone Roses to Slade. It was a rush of British rock and pop heritage. Twelve songs that would go on to inspire countless kids on council estates across the country to pick up guitars and start playing. Twelve songs that showed how easy it was to be a rock 'n' roll star - all you needed was the look, the attitude, the songs, the ability and, if you could find them, two bona fide geniuses. Easy.

> *'In 20 years' time our album Definitely Maybe will still be in the shops and that's what it's about. In 20 years' time people will buy the album and listen to it for what it is. They won't listen to it because we were rock 'n' roll or something like that. That's what matters.'*
>
> (Noel Gallagher)

Noel is right, of course, people don't keep buying his new records, or Liam's, because of their 'rock 'n' roll' behaviour and it's not why people are still buying and listening to 'Definitely Maybe'. That is purely down to the brilliance of the songs. It would be naive though to ignore the fact that the sibling (wibling?) rivalry between Noel and Liam has been a central part of the Oasis story and that for people on the fringes of popular music (the sort of people who buy Coldplay albums) it is the largest part of the story. You can't blame Liam or Noel for that, but it remains true.

Lots of families have feuds and lots of brothers don't get on and so the significance of the battles between the Gallagher boys isn't because they are unique in any way but is because they have happened in the full view of the public and because the UK tabloid press make every effort to stoke the flames. Oh and it's also because of cocaine. I think that once again we have to return to their childhood to find reasons for the bitterness that sometimes defines their relationship. No doubt both Noel and Liam would dismiss that as bullshit and psycho-babble (and they may be right) but there is some discussion in the psychology community about the negative impact that domestic violence can have on sibling relationships. Academics at the University of Memphis have carried out some research into this (as have others) and they certainly believe that witnessing violence in the home can have very many negative consequences.

For a while the antics of the band threatened to get in the way of the music. Brawls on ferries, aborted gigs, drink and drugs all made great copy but also hinted that, much like so many other bands who arrive with a bang, they would ultimately be destined to go out with a whimper. However, what nobody knew at that point was that Noel and Liam were only just warming up.

Oasis' arrival and the massive success of 'Definitely Maybe' had a devastating impact on popular culture. While it is undeniably a great album, the truth is that it was also the signal for the end of the line for indie music - and that was what Britpop really was, a gaggle of bands who, a decade earlier, would never have caught the attention of major labels or television but who thanks to a wave of nostalgia, the death of Kurt Cobain and the desire for something to believe in had become genuine pop stars. Jarvis Cocker and Pulp had been releasing records since 1983 without anyone ever knowing they existed. Saint Etienne's 'Fox Base Alpha' had just scraped into the top forty albums in 1991. Anyone who thinks that Suede would have enjoyed the same sort of success if they had arrived in 1986 is delusional. Britpop from the very start was about art school aesthetics, effeminate boys, charity shop clothes and cult television and film.

Oasis erased all of that within six months and ushered in something very different, something less delicate and something much uglier too.

In an early season of the British comedy 'Peep Show', Mark (David Mitchell) is trying to worm his way back into the affections of 'the one', Sophie (Olivia Colman), who is now dating the boorish and boring Jeff (Neil Fitzmaurice). To win Sophie back, Mark decides he has to befriend Jeff and so he meets him in a local 'boozer' to play snooker and drink pints. In preparation he commits to memory some stories from a 'lads' mag - one about a shepherd who eats his own testicles and something about a sexy woman. It is painful to watch someone so defiantly not a lad try so desperately to be one. Everything about Mark reveals that he doesn't belong in Jeff's world, in particular his clothes, the way he holds himself and his obvious discomfort with the vulgarity of the conversation that he is attempting to steer.

When Britpop first reared its head it was a Mark Corrigan. A bit awkward. Slightly old fashioned. Eager to please and to find favour with a mainstream audience. Dressed up in a tank top and Farah slacks. The music was articulate, delicate and fun (I know, the fun bit is where the Corrigan metaphor falls apart) and it appealed directly to the likes of me. I couldn't play snooker, I found looking at 'sexy birds' in magazines uncomfortable (reading 'The Female Eunuch' at thirteen probably didn't help here) and I was never *ever* one of the lads.

I see a lot of the Britpop bands that I adore as being Corrigans, with a little dash of his slightly more adventurous and much more stupid flatmate, Jeremy (Robert Webb) at crucial moments. But none of them were ever Jeff. Jeff's idea of a great conversation was to talk about Jeremy's trainers; he liked to ridicule and belittle people he perceived as weaker than himself and he thought nothing about calling a woman a 'freak'. He was, in short, ugly.

The 'Jeffs' arrive later in the Britpop story. They read Loaded, they would have found the idea of a Turkish shepherd eating his own testicles hilarious, they adored the Manics for the line about only wanting to get drunk and not for the idea that libraries might give us power. The key Jeffpop moment comes when Noel Gallagher stated 'I hate that Alex and Damon. I hope they catch AIDS and die.' Interestingly that quote comes in at number one in an article entitled '10 Hilarious Noel Gallagher Quotes'.

To really understand the Jeffing of Britpop listen to The Verve's 'A Northern Soul', or any of the songs that preceded it. At this point Richard Ashcroft reveals himself as a poet with a lot to say about male fragility and mental health. Watch the way he holds himself on stage, the way he presents himself, confident but never cocky, an eccentric. He was at this point a quasi-spiritual figure, cut through with a certain vulnerability and air of humanity. The music is just as much of a swirl, a *maelstrom*, of emotion as the lyrics were. Then watch the video for 'Bitter Sweet Symphony' with Ashcroft barrelling his way through the streets, knocking over women and mimicking the Gallagher trademark 'swagger'. Gone is the vulnerability that drew people like me to The Verve, and in its place has appeared a man who laughs at Turkish shepherds. Just another Jeff.

It is difficult to separate the rise of Oasis from the emergence of lad culture. Oasis were lads and their audience was primarily made up of lads (or boys who wanted to act like lads so that the real lads would leave them alone) and they completely changed the look, sound and, crucially, soul of what Britpop had been up until their arrival.

Shortly before the release of 'Definitely Maybe', Loaded, a new magazine aimed at 'men who should know better' was launched. The first issue landed in May 1994 and featured Gary Oldman on the front cover and articles about Paul Weller, Eric Cantona and 'Beavis and Butthead' inside. Mundane but harmless stuff. But the December issue that followed the release of 'Definitely Maybe' was a more revealing insight into what the magazine was actually about and where the Britpop and the Cool Britannia brand was heading.

The cover featured a picture of Kathy Lloyd in a basque and suspenders with the accompanying tag-line of 'Britain's hottest babe.' This was the top shelf world of Playboy and Mayfair packaged up with a slice of irony that very few of the target audience cared about. It was, and there is no way to escape it, porn. This was very soft core for sure but it was, nevertheless, the sort of reductive, politically incorrect and sexist imagery, attitude and iconography that the indie music scene had railed against just twelve months earlier. Here was the 'To-be-looked-at-ness' that Laura Mulvey had exposed in her seminal 1973 work 'Visual and Other Pleasures'.

The link between Loaded and Oasis may seem tenuous but that quip wishing AIDS on members of Blur is, at best, evidence of a less than pleasant attitude to the gay community and, at worst, is just violently homophobic. The implication was clear - Blur were 'a bit gay' and Oasis were 'real men'. Loaded was the lad bible and Oasis were the lad band.

The follow up to 'Definitely Maybe', '(What's the Story) Morning Glory' would arrive in October 1995 and it was, despite its supernova success, a tired, tiresome and tedious work. Full of bromidic anthems like 'Don't Look Back in Anger' and threadbare Status Quo-alike singles like 'Roll With It', which is only narrowly pipped to the post for worst single of the era by Blur's 'Country House'. The energy and vitality, the sneering attitude and the punk sensibility of the debut had been replaced by something that had seemingly been factory manufactured (if only it had been Factory manufactured) to appeal to middle-aged, middle-class, middle-of-the-road types with disposable income to spend on music at the checkout as they did the weekly big shop.

The cheery, cheeky, delights and charms of 'Parklife', the sex and charity shop chic of 'Suede' and the post-punk style of 'Elastica' were replaced by the drone of 'Wonderwall'. The success of 'Morning Glory' led to A&R men instantly ditching their desire to find the next Suede so that they could hit the North to find any four blokes in Stone Island with a copy of 'Rubber Soul' to throw a record contract at.

Evidence of this shift in focus can be found in the fact that in December 1994 the legendary boss of Sire, Seymour Stein flew from his home in the USA to catch a set from a band called Lick. Lick were fronted by the openly gay Gary Cosby, an Australian who had fled his home in Australia to chase his dreams of becoming a star like Suzi Quatro. Lick had songs with titles like 'Come' and 'Shirtlifter'. They were, very definitely, *not* lads. In a message to people in Sire's London offices, Stein had this to say: *'Really glad I mustered up the strength to overcome jet-lag and see Lick on Saturday night. Once they were on stage I forgot that I was tired... couldn't get the music out of my head and was up until well past 3 a.m... please DO NOT LOSE THIS DEAL.'* Lick got a deal but their album has never been released, which can be put down to the fact that they didn't sound, or behave, like Oasis.

The shadow that Oasis cast over British music and the nation's wider culture was long and, at times, darker than many people would care to acknowledge or accept. There is an argument that says criticising them is a form of snobbery, that you are targeting them because they are working class. That may well be true for

Right: "Manchester kids have the best record collections", Tony Wilson. (Image by Ash Loydon)

Below: "Popscene" (30 March 1992) is widely regarded as the starting point for what would become Britpop.

Left: "Parklife" (25 April 1994) is one of the defining records of the Britpop era and the one that made Blur genuine pop stars. (Image by Ash Loydon)

Below: "The Drowners" (11 May 1992) the debut single from Suede.

Right: "Britpop was a laddish, distasteful, misogynistic, nationalistic cartoon." (Brett Anderson, October 2019, BBC "Hardtalk")

Below: "Stutter" (1 November 1993) a glorious hymn to erectile dysfunction.

Left: Justine Frischmann, lead singer of Elastica, is arguably the central figure in the Britpop tale with links to both Suede and Blur as well as her band's own output. (Image by Ash Loydon)

Below: "D'you Know What I Mean" (7 July 1997) While Oasis may never truly have been a Britpop band, their part in the story of "Cool Britannia" and enduring legacy cannot be denied.

Right: If Britpop were an episode of "Peep Show", Oasis would be Jeff. (Image by Ash Loydon)

Below: "Common People" (22 May 1995) one of the defining moments of the Britpop era is Pulp's headline slot at Glastonbury in 1995 when "Common People" united 80,000 people in a field.

SIDE A   **Common People**
          Pulp

220595

Left: Arch, camp, soaked in kitchen sink drama and kitsch, Pulp were the blueprint for the sound and look of much of the Britpop period. (Image by Ash Loydon)

Below: "Delicious" (9 May 1994) Lead singer, Louise Wener, was one of the most intelligent and articulate artists of the era and stubbornly refused to fulfil the role of "woman in rock" that so many journalists wanted her to.

With 8 consecutive top 40 hit singles, four top twenty albums and countless front covers, Sleeper were one of the most important and successful bands of the era. (Image by Ash Loydon)

Lad culture, which would be better described as misogyny, was a central part of "Cool Britannia" and was given physical form by journals like "Loaded". (Image by Ash Loydon)

Left: Few bands better capture the impact of Oasis and Lad Culture than The Verve who shifted from sensitive, shamanic, psych-rocker to stadium trad-rock in the space of a single album. (Image by Ash Loydon)

Below: "Bellyache E.P" (November 1993).

Literate and political, Echobelly's Sonya Madan was a radical and inspiring figure. (Image by Ash Loydon)

"Disappointed" (1994) is, arguably, the great "lost" single of the period.

"For the Dead" (May 1994).

Fronted by Martin "Rozzer" Rossiter, Gene were often compared to The Smiths but, in truth, those comparisons were down to the fact that Rossiter, like Morrissey, had a neat line in witticisms. (Image by Ash Loydon)

Lick frontman, Gary Cosby, was one of the few openly gay performers in Britpop. The band's playful imagery and provocative titles and lyrics were a joy.

"The Young Own the Town" (20 November 1995).

Right: Soda, from Hull, had the world at their feet before tragedy struck. Their long lost album "Artificial Flavour" was finally released in 2017. (Image by Ash Loydon)

Below: "Violent Men" (30 May 1994).

Bands like Marion, Strangelove, The Longpigs and Elcka all drew inspiration from the darker corners of the Britpop room. Tales of domestic violence, sex and sexuality, isolation and identity made them the natural heirs to the likes of The Smiths. Music for box room rebels and the grotesquely lonely.

"12 Reasons Why I Love Her" (August 1996).

"Inelegantly Wasted in Papa's Penthouse Pad in Belgravia" (3 July 1995).

Above: "No Time" (1994).

Left: Photo of the author and his younger brother at the height of the Britpop era.

the look, sound and, crucially, soul of what Britpop had been up until their arrival.

Shortly before the release of 'Definitely Maybe', Loaded, a new magazine aimed at 'men who should know better' was launched. The first issue landed in May 1994 and featured Gary Oldman on the front cover and articles about Paul Weller, Eric Cantona and 'Beavis and Butthead' inside. Mundane but harmless stuff. But the December issue that followed the release of 'Definitely Maybe' was a more revealing insight into what the magazine was actually about and where the Britpop and the Cool Britannia brand was heading.

The cover featured a picture of Kathy Lloyd in a basque and suspenders with the accompanying tag-line of 'Britain's hottest babe.' This was the top shelf world of Playboy and Mayfair packaged up with a slice of irony that very few of the target audience cared about. It was, and there is no way to escape it, porn. This was very soft core for sure but it was, nevertheless, the sort of reductive, politically incorrect and sexist imagery, attitude and iconography that the indie music scene had railed against just twelve months earlier. Here was the 'To-be-looked-at-ness' that Laura Mulvey had exposed in her seminal 1973 work 'Visual and Other Pleasures'.

The link between Loaded and Oasis may seem tenuous but that quip wishing AIDS on members of Blur is, at best, evidence of a less than pleasant attitude to the gay community and, at worst, is just violently homophobic. The implication was clear - Blur were 'a bit gay' and Oasis were 'real men'. Loaded was the lad bible and Oasis were the lad band.

The follow up to 'Definitely Maybe', '(What's the Story) Morning Glory' would arrive in October 1995 and it was, despite its supernova success, a tired, tiresome and tedious work. Full of bromidic anthems like 'Don't Look Back in Anger' and threadbare Status Quo-alike singles like 'Roll With It', which

is only narrowly pipped to the post for worst single of the era by Blur's 'Country House'. The energy and vitality, the sneering attitude and the punk sensibility of the debut had been replaced by something that had seemingly been factory manufactured (if only it had been Factory manufactured) to appeal to middle-aged, middle-class, middle-of-the-road types with disposable income to spend on music at the checkout as they did the weekly big shop.

The cheery, cheeky, delights and charms of 'Parklife', the sex and charity shop chic of 'Suede' and the post-punk style of 'Elastica' were replaced by the drone of 'Wonderwall'. The success of 'Morning Glory' led to A&R men instantly ditching their desire to find the next Suede so that they could hit the North to find any four blokes in Stone Island with a copy of 'Rubber Soul' to throw a record contract at.

Evidence of this shift in focus can be found in the fact that in December 1994 the legendary boss of Sire, Seymour Stein flew from his home in the USA to catch a set from a band called Lick. Lick were fronted by the openly gay Gary Cosby, an Australian who had fled his home in Australia to chase his dreams of becoming a star like Suzi Quatro. Lick had songs with titles like 'Come' and 'Shirtlifter'. They were, very definitely, *not* lads. In a message to people in Sire's London offices, Stein had this to say: *'Really glad I mustered up the strength to overcome jet-lag and see Lick on Saturday night. Once they were on stage I forgot that I was tired... couldn't get the music out of my head and was up until well past 3 a.m... please DO NOT LOSE THIS DEAL.'* Lick got a deal but their album has never been released, which can be put down to the fact that they didn't sound, or behave, like Oasis.

The shadow that Oasis cast over British music and the nation's wider culture was long and, at times, darker than many people would care to acknowledge or accept. There is an argument that says criticising them is a form of snobbery, that you are targeting them because they are working class. That may well be true for

some of the privately educated music critics at certain newspapers, but it isn't true of me. I grew up in a working class home, I know about poverty, both financial and in relation to aspiration, and I know the challenges and scars it creates in your life. But to suggest that working class culture can only be boorish, macho, violent and backward looking is the real snobbery. Oasis are a great rock band, they produced an astonishing debut album, they dominated the cultural landscape like no other band since The Beatles and they inspired legions of kids to pick up a guitar and start writing songs but, crucially, they are the antithesis of what Britpop was. That's the story, mourning glory.

Chapter 7

Northern Souls

The Verve

This is the tale of some Northern souls.

Floating like butterflies across a storm in Heaven.

Singing urban hymns.

Heading forth because they were not prepared to simply sit and wonder.

Born without a silver spoon.

They were The Verve.

Wigan is the home to one of the most unusual youth subcultures in British history. Northern Soul was a strange mix of trainspotter obsession, hedonism, dancing and, most important, a belief in the power of music to transport you from the humdrum town where the rain seems to fall hard every day.

The Wigan Casino was the Mecca of this movement, where coach loads of kids armed with talcum powder, speed, patches and dance moves inspired by Bruce Lee as opposed to Fred Astaire would dance from the moment the needle dropped on the first single until the needle lifted from the last many, many hours later.

It put Wigan at the very heart of a scene that took its inspiration from Mod and would be the inspiration for the rave culture of the 1990s. Wigan burned bright in those days and was a beacon to kids from all across the country who just wanted to be free, to have a good time and to get loaded.

By the time the 1990s arrived, Wigan, like so many towns across the north of England, was in the grip of seemingly never ending economic decline with unemployment, crime and social exclusion having replaced the good times, good tunes and giddy highs of those Northern Soul years.

Oscar Wilde said that 'Nothing should be beyond hope - life is hope.'

Hope was in short supply in the North, as it had been replaced with something much more troubling and potentially fatal: hopelessness.

When Richard Ashcroft was eleven years old, his father died suddenly of a brain haemorrhage. The death of a parent in childhood is a traumatic event which can have several negative impacts on the child including the increased likelihood of substance abuse, a higher risk of unemployment and underachievement at school and a greater likelihood of depression and other mental health issues. Of course there are things that can help to reduce such negative outcomes but it's not too fanciful to see some aspects of the person we 'know' as Richard Ashcroft as being shaped by this unhappy childhood experience.

At some point following this trauma his mother remarried and Richard was introduced to the ideas of Rosicrucianism - a form of spiritual, esoteric thinking and belief that has its origins in the early 17th century. According to the writer Carl Lindgren, the doctrine of the movement is built on 'esoteric truths' that 'provide insight...into nature, the physical universe and the spiritual realm', all of which sounds exactly like the sort of thing Richard Ashcroft was talking about in interviews in the 1990s.

When he reached Winstanley Sixth Form College Ashcroft started a band called Verve with Nick McCabe, Simon Jones and Peter Salisbury. This early incarnation of the band played their first gig at an 18th birthday party at the Honeysuckle in Wigan. Soon after that they were signed by Hut and released their first offerings to the public in the shape of 'All in the Mind', 'She's a Superstar' and 'Gravity'. They were psychedelic, experimental and highlighted the considerable talents of McCabe as a musician and Ashcroft as a strange, compelling and shamanic lead singer. All three of those singles made it to the top of the independent charts and 'She's a Superstar' made it into the top 75 of the singles charts.

The scene was set for their debut album. 'A Storm in Heaven' was released in 1993 and enjoyed not inconsiderable success, reaching number twenty-seven in the charts. These were the very earliest moments of Britpop so it wasn't surprising to see the lead single from the album, 'Blue', only reaching number sixty nine in the charts. The real success of the album though was the fact that it led to support slots with another relatively unknown Northern band called Oasis. They also supported Smashing Pumpkins on their 'Siamese Dreams' European tour, which exposed them to a much wider audience, although having to spend time with Billy Corgan was a heavy price to pay for that.

I was reading the NME and Melody Maker every week at this point in time and I was buying a lot of records but for some reason, The Verve simply passed me by. I feel like I really missed out on something. 'A Storm in Heaven' is a really great record, it's full of swirling guitars, heartfelt vocals, and enigmatic lyrics and oozes a confidence that is matched by the music. I think I could have become a bit evangelical about The Verve if I'd heard it at that point, while 'Blue' would have broken the stylus on my turntable through multiple plays - seriously, go and listen to it now and then tell me honestly if you managed to resist the temptation to play it again as soon as it finished.

1994 saw the band build on the modest success of 'A Storm in Heaven' with a slot on the Lollapalooza tour in the US. It was here that the first signs of the troubles that lay at the heart of Richard Ashcroft and The Verve as a whole began to seep into the wider world. Ashcroft was treated for dehydration following a lengthy drinking session, Pete Salisbury was arrested for trashing a hotel room while under the influence of drugs and later Richard remembered: 'America nearly killed us'.

However, out of the madness and turmoil came a set of songs that, despite not being as commercially successful as 'Urban Hymns', are the very best that The Verve ever recorded. Those songs were gathered together as 'A Northern Soul', which is one of the greatest ever albums by a British band, which deserves its place alongside the very best of British popular music and arrived in 1995 to a world that was ready, willing and able to receive it.

The album opens with 'A New Decade' and it is instantly clear that we are not dealing with the pop thrills of the brighter side of the nascent Britpop scene. Lyrically it involves the sort of brutal honesty that is sadly lacking in so much music. Ashcroft reveals all of his demons and makes no attempt to hide behind carefully constructed and clever lyrical tricks - he simply lays himself bare and does so with an air of confidence that suggests he really doesn't care what you, or anyone else, might think of him. A few years earlier this sort of song would have been wrapped up in jingling, jangling guitars and would have been sung by someone for whom the description 'fey and winsome' would have been the only option. Not here though - instead the music swirls and swells, even roars at times and the vocals are forceful, wilful and assured.

The first record that I ever owned by The Verve was 'This is Music'. I bought it as a CD single from HMV in the Wellgate Shopping Centre in Dundee when I should have been hawking Coca-Cola to shopkeepers on the Lochee Road. When I got back to my little Vauxhall Combo van I put the single into the CD player and waited to hear what the fuss was all about. Three and a half minutes later I understood entirely.

A tambourine shakes and shimmies, a bass line that threatens to pulp your bones pulsates, a guitar howls with more rage than

Ginsberg and then, once again, there is that voice, punching itself into your ears before it shatters your brain. The opening line is, perhaps, the final word on the British class system.

In a better world than this one 'This is Music' would sit at the top table along with the likes of 'Live Forever', 'Girls and Boys' and 'Common People' as one of the defining singles of the times and there's no real reason why it doesn't - or at least there is no *good* reason. It's possibly too real, too serious, too heavy and too intense to capture the prevailing mood of the times but what it *does* capture is the righteous indignation of a band feverishly grabbing at their chance to be heard.

The second single from the album was 'On Your Own' a song that is a hymn to the pain of loneliness, an ode to the fragility and temporary nature of this thing we call life and a plea for someone or something to fill the hole in our soul.

At the risk of sounding 'soft', I cried the first time I listened to this.

I cried the second time too.

I've cried at other times when I've heard it.

I'm listening to it as I write this and I can feel the tears welling.

I'm not ashamed.

Sometimes I feel very lonely.

I worry about my place in this world.

I feel sure I'm not doing things right.

What if I'm not doing 'husband' right?

What if I'm not doing 'dad' right?

I'm all too familiar with the terrifying prospect of this life being all there is - of it being a fleeting series of moments that, if we get them wrong, can have terrible and terrifying consequences for others long after we have gone.

I've got to get rid of this hole inside.

You know, right?

It's not just me.

I'm not alone of course.

I love.

I am loved.

It's good to have a song that understands those moments of doubt, fear and worry. Good to feel that someone, somewhere, sometime has felt the same way and survived.

The third single from the album is 'History' which is a confident, fragile, swaggering, tender, heartbreaking and heartfelt song of love and the loss of love. It's also a song that returns, again, to the transient nature of life and, indeed, love.

Brothers and sisters, Richard Ashcroft is a poet and a lyricist to match any of the others that we place on pedestals and hail as geniuses.

The main difference between Ashcroft and certain other Northern writers who have addressed the human condition, is that they were mostly art school sorts, or the sorts that art school sorts liked - pale faced, wan and convinced that there was nothing more to life than books. Ashcroft sang his songs like a rock star - he looked like a rock star, he had more confidence than a room full of Liam Gallaghers, he was threatening and, gasp, he took loads of drugs. The heart of Morrissey coupled with the appetite of Keith Richards.

'A Northern Soul' broke into the top twenty, peaking at number thirteen, and eventually went Gold. If 'A Storm in Heaven' had politely hinted this was a band who deserved to have attention paid to them, then 'A Northern Soul' put the niceties to one side and *demanded* you pay attention and then, when you had, ordered you to bend the knee in supplication.

The Verve were here.

Except they were actually *not*.

A few weeks before 'History' was released, the band split up for the first time. Ashcroft later explained that he had been unhappy enough to want to break the band up at an earlier point.

Despite the fact that 'History' took them higher and further than anything else up to that point and despite the fact that no longer existing as an active enterprise at that point may well have cost them their shot, he remains convinced it was the right decision.

> *'I knew that I had to do it earlier on, but I just wouldn't face it. Once you're not happy in anything, there's no point living in it, is there? But my addiction to playing and writing and being in this band was so great that I wouldn't do anything about it. It felt awful because it could have been the greatest time of our lives, with 'History' doing well, but I still think I can look myself in the mirror in 30 years time and say, 'Yeah man, you did the right thing.' The others had been through the same thing. It was a mixture of sadness and regret, and relief that we would have some time away.'*[1]

The split only lasted for a few weeks and when they reunited it was without Nick McCabe. A short experiment with former Suede guitarist Bernard Butler only lasted a few days before finally they recruited former school friend Simon Tong and set about writing and recording new material. Eventually, in 1997, McCabe returned to the fold and the stage was set for their first new album in two years.

1997 was the year when Britpop became the mainstream and not just a part of the mainstream, which also means that it was the beginning of the end. By 1998, the entire movement would be crumbling under the weight of bored record companies looking for the next big thing, cocaine, the horror that was Cool Britannia and the dawning realisation that the tidal wave of joy that we all

---

1. Dark Star, 2010

thought we were riding like Bodhi in 'Point Break'[2] was, in fact, a splash in the bathtub of popular culture.

Never mind though, because in 1997 we were able to enjoy the 'New' Labour election victory, Dolly the sheep, the launch of Channel 5, the first Harry Potter book, the IRA declaring a ceasefire, 'Candle in the Wind' being at number one forever, the Queen's fiftieth wedding anniversary and Tom Finney getting a knighthood - and The Verve released 'Urban Hymns'.

June 1997 brought a brand new single from The Verve and, once again, a subtle change in the style, feel and sound of the music. Between the psychedelic rock of 'A Storm in Heaven' to the alternative rock of 'A Northern Soul' they had modified, moderated and moulded the sound and now, yet again, they were doing things slightly differently, while remaining, still, recognisably them.

The single was 'Bitter Sweet Symphony' and it remains, arguably, the song by The Verve that elevated them from a band on the fringes of mainstream success and mass adoration to a band who were destined to fill stadiums and take their place alongside Oasis as one of the great rock 'n' roll acts of the 20th century and possibly beyond. Built around a sample of the Andrew Loog Oldham orchestral version of The Rolling Drones'[3] 'The Last Time' the song is a perfect moment in rock and pop history.

As strings begin to swell with that now impossible not to recognise coda, electronic tweets join in, drums begin to gently beat and then the voice and the words. Once again Ashcroft returns to the theme of isolation and heartache, proving, again, that he was more than just the 'Mad Richard' derided by the press for his

---

2. 1991 Kathryn Bigelow film starring Keanu Reeves and Patrick Swayze about a cop who goes undercover in the world of surfers to apprehend a gang of bank robbers - no, really.
3. I know it's petty to take these cheap shots at aging rockers but I just can't help myself.

claims of being able to fly[4] and his pseudo-spiritual musings. Yes, he was, and let's just be honest, indeed a madman - but he was also a maddening genius.

The song was everywhere. Now The Verve were in the top ten, on Top of the Pops and the front cover of the NME like proper rock stars, which was exactly where they wanted to be. Actually, they were one step away from where they wanted to be, because 'Bitter Sweet Symphony' only made it to number two in the charts.

So close.

Yet so far away.

Thankfully they had a response to that - they released a second single from the, as yet unreleased, third album in the shape of 'The Drugs Don't Work', which *did* make it to number one and confirmed their status as one of the biggest bands in the country.

'Urban Hymns' couldn't fail. 'Urban Hymns' *didn't* fail. Eventually it would go platinum eleven times in the UK. It was an enormous hit everywhere in the world, including in the USA where it sold over one million copies and where the singles were on near constant rotation on alternative rock stations throughout the year.

Then it all began to unravel again. After the highs of reaching number one and a massive gig at Haigh Hall in front of over thirty thousand people, they found themselves touring Europe where, after a gig in Germany, there was what is politely referred to as an 'incident' involving Nick McCabe and Richard Ashcroft. That incident left McCabe with a broken hand and Tricky Dicky with a sore face.

McCabe left, and it's very easy to understand why he made that decision. Drink and drugs were a big part of The Verve 'experience' and wherever you find those things you inevitably

---

4. In a 1992 interview Ashcroft stated 'I believe you can fly and I believe in Astral Travel'. The drugs do work.

find chaos. McCabe had had enough of the chaos and the madness and who could blame him?

The band carried on, but it wasn't the same band. Not just because of the departure of McCabe but because the chaos had replaced the fire. Madness had taken over from inspiration. They were a shadow of what they had been and, inevitably, things came to an end in April 1999. A sad end to something that had been, briefly, so magnificent.

In 2007 they returned, without Simon Tong, and reunited for a series of sold out shows across the UK and a new album 'Forth' which, while a fine collection of songs, failed to do anything to heal the wounds of the past. McCabe and Jones felt that Ashcroft had used the whole exercise to promote and reinvigorate his own solo aspirations and, once again, the band were over within a year. While there has been no official split announcement it was obvious that The Verve, as any meaningful entity, were over *again*.

The story of The Verve is full of all the elements that feature in most rock 'n' roll stories - grandiose claims of brilliance, arrogance, swagger, cool clothes, drink and drug fuelled excess, big hits, open warfare between members and blah, blah, blah but what sets The Verve apart from being, as Scroobius Pip[5] would have it, 'just a band' is Ashcroft's ability as a writer. Few, if any, of the bands who really hit big in the nineties dealt with the issues he felt able to tackle and those that did didn't do so with the same level of naked, brutal honesty that he brought to the table. He was more than a songwriter, he was a man who was documenting the bitterness of life, the pain in our hearts and the emptiness in our souls.

---

5. English poet, spoken word performer and podcaster who released the single 'Thou Shalt Always Kill' with Dan le Sac in 2007. The song features a long list of bands who are sacred cows with their names being followed by the chant of 'Just a band'.

It would have been a more interesting and rewarding story had they not fallen into the middle of the road with the likes of Oasis, Cast and Ocean Colour Scene, making records that sounded anthemic in a stadium but that lacked any real emotional weight or spiritual depth. You can blame record label pressure, you can blame cocaine or you can blame fame itself but the decision to be a rock band places The Verve on the same level as a lot of other underwhelming bands, when 'A Northern Soul' seemed to promise something so much more and so much better than that.

Chapter 8

We Want to Get Loaded?

'It says here that she claims she had journalists interview her just because they fancied her... I don't want you to think that's the case this evening, I want you to know it's the case this evening.'

That was Chris Evans [1] opening gambit in his interview with Louise Wener on TFI Friday [2] in June 1996.

The opening gambit.

Not even so much as a 'How are you?' before the aggressive 'flirting' and objectifying began. Not that that would have made it any better. It's terribly uncomfortable to watch *anyone* hitting on someone else so aggressively. This isn't a coy glance or a slowly emerging chemistry between two adults. This is just a fairly awful man letting a woman know that he wants to go to bed with her.

He went on to make some fairly lurid remarks about the fact that Louise was no longer in a relationship with her bandmate Jon but was now dating the drummer Andy, which led Evans to suggest that she was 'working her way through' the men in the band and was 'having the time of your life'.

Cor.

Phwoar.

---

1. British broadcaster who, in the nineties, was on television almost constantly.
2. Channel 4, Friday night music and chat show which featured many performances from Britpop stars.

Fast forward six years and Wener is being interviewed by another 'bloke' on television. This time she is not 'just' a pop star, she is a published author and a serious figure.

Surely, this time the interview will focus on her talents as a writer. Surely, this time, in a new decade, the approach will be less loaded, or indeed Loaded, and more careful.

Nope.

The interviewer Ralf Little[3], Anthony from 'The Royle Family', decided it was entirely appropriate to share his wanton teenage fantasies about Louise and to let everyone know about her role in his onanism.

Vile.

Because she knew the rules of engagement Louise tried hard to maintain a veneer of quiet amusement but I'm fairly confident that having men speak to you in this manner, and doing so in front of thousands of strangers, must be very draining.

Exhausting.

It would be lovely to think that things have improved.

They haven't.

Every day on Twitter, or in certain newspapers, women are rounded on, hounded, attacked and brutalised for the clothes they have chosen to wear, for their weight, their hair, their 'hotness' or otherwise. At the risk of upsetting people who don't understand that being kind is a sign of strength and not weakness, it is ugly and when you support it, that makes you ugly too.

When Wener guested on a track with The Lottery Winners in February 2021, one blogger decided that the highest praise he could offer was to tell everyone that Louise Wener was 'getting me hot under my jim jams this morning.' What makes this so awful is that he @-ed her in the post. Nearly three decades on from the very worst aspects of Britpop and yet some people

---

3. The Ralf Little Show, BBC One, 2002

haven't taken a single step forward. What that 'writer' was saying was 'Hey, Louise, you've given me an erection.' He's not alone of course, the world is full of crashing bores who think that reducing female artists to their 'hotness' is perfectly fine. They will bow down, bend the knee and doff their bucket hat at whichever rock star in a Stone Island parka manages to spew out something that sounds a bit like The Beatles and never mention how much heat is being generated in their jimjams. Funny that. I'm no radical feminist, I may not even be a feminist depending on who you speak to, but I have a radical solution to this sort of ugliness - just stop it.

It isn't just Louise Wener who is subjected to this sort of thing. Not very long ago, I overheard someone at a Britpop gig bellow that they had to get to the front of the crowd to catch Salad in action because 'She's a hotty'. Marijne van der Vlugt has been a model, a television presenter, a singer, a writer and a performer for thirty years. But that all takes second place to how attractive, or otherwise, the middle-aged men trapped in their extended adolescence believe her to be. You could hear the same things being said about Sonya Madan, Saffron of Republica, Lauren Laverne, Justine Frischmann or any of the other women who were a key part of Britpop. Hearing those things in 1996 from the mouths of boys is one thing but hearing them today from the mouths of men is something else.

The contribution of these female artists is a central part of the Britpop story and not because of how big my, or your, crush on them was. It's because, for possibly the first time in British guitar music history, they were front and centre as writers, musicians and performers. They inspired young women, they helped young men like me to think about our attitudes and they made some of the most important records of the era.

It's impossible to talk about any of this without mentioning Loaded of course.

The louder a man brays about his feminist credentials the more convinced I become that a nasty story involving gaslighting, abuse, assault or worse is looming. This seems particularly true when the man involved is touched, tainted by the fickle finger of fame in some way. Sinister men have always used feminism as just another means of using and abusing women.

Because I was raised in a religious home I never participated in the 'locker room' talk of my peers - sex was a sacred thing that was to be enjoyed only within the confines of marriage and women were to be respected with both words and deeds Also, it just hasn't ever really sat particularly well with me as that sort of boorishness and lad culture always seemed a bit, well, *crass* and demeaning. For both boys *and* girls. The fact that I didn't drink also helped me avoid becoming one of those boys as beer turns lots of men into *blokes*.

Spending your adolescence at church or in your bedroom reading Edith Sitwell and Shelagh Delaney doesn't really equip you for joining in with the 'lads' as they leer and catcall 'birds'. When a boy in my class at school performed an unspeakable act of naughtiness with a girl on the floor of her parents' kitchen, while they were away for the weekend, I was at home watching 'The Leather Boys' on VHS and wondering what Morrissey was up to.

This probably makes my decision to go all in on Loaded during the Britpop years all the more startling, astonishing, depressing? It didn't last long really. But for a few months I bought it, read it and then pinned the posters of various celebrity women in various stages of undress onto the walls of my digs at university.

I can remember a friend coming over to visit after this had been going on for a few months and looking at the wall, then looking at me, then back at the wall and then just shaking his head. He was older and smarter and he saw it for what it was: cheap thrills, soft porn, exploitation (of the women and me) and a bit, let's be honest, tawdry.

I get it.

I hear your arguments.

'He's only saying this stuff to make himself look virtuous.'

This is, at least in part, true. I *do* want to paint a picture of myself that is virtuous but it's not accurate. I have behaved as abysmally as the next person in my life. I am no saint. I've cheated, lied, betrayed, hurt and been just plain unpleasant on far more occasions than I have not been those things. I am, like most people, flawed and a little bit broken. I am not placing myself on the moral high ground. I am just trying to examine why it is that I would have allowed myself to be dragged into a fairly unpleasant alleyway off the main street of Britpop.

I have often railed against the portrayal of Britpop, particularly from the righteous brethren and sisters of the Guardian, as being xenophobic (at best) and sexist.

That wasn't my experience. My experience of Britpop was of seeing people from places in society that I had no previous knowledge of suddenly taking a place in my heart and on my walls as heroes, icons and inspiration.

Yet despite all of that I still fell for the Loaded moment. I don't think that I was smart enough to defend myself by wielding the mighty sword of irony. I think I just really wanted to belong. I had spent a long time on the outside and now Britpop had dragged people like me inside, but from despair to where?

I should have stuck to the sage advice from The Kinks, that I'm not like everybody else. But we all want to be like everybody else. We all want to belong. We all want to be *someone*. Even if that someone is actually trying to be someone else. Looking back now I feel a bit icky when I think about what I was putting on my walls.

When Loaded arrived in May 1994 it all looked fairly innocent with bad boy actor Gary Oldman mimicking an old shot of Michael Caine (a Loaded favourite) along with articles on Paul Weller and Eric Cantona. Plus there was the promise of something a bit naughty with an article on hotel sex. Given that I wasn't having *any* sex I was prepared to go along with it.

All innocent enough.

The strap-line hints at what is to come though doesn't it? 'For men who should know better'.

Just three months later the front cover of Loaded didn't feature an iconic actor, instead it had two 'naughty sorts' in football shirts giving come hither looks to the camera in a way that wasn't all that far away from page three. What is wrong with two independent young women making a choice to model like this? Get back in the fifties, granddad. Mary Whitehouse called. I get it. I do. Girl power. I just wonder how much choice is actually being exercised and how much manipulation and coercion is taking place?

There are people far better placed to comment on that than me of course. I'm just thinking.

Laura Mulvey couldn't have imagined such a thing when she wrote about the 'male gaze'.

> 'In a world ordered by sexual imbalance, pleasure in looking has been split between active/male and passive/female. The determining male gaze projects its phantasy on to the female form which is styled accordingly. In their traditional exhibitionist role women are simultaneously looked at and displayed, with their appearance coded for strong visual and erotic impact so that they can be said to connote to-be-looked-at-ness.'
>
> (Visual and Other Pleasures, Laura Mulvey)

The women on the cover of Loaded were not being presented to us as they would wish. They were being presented to us as men wish them to be.

What happens to the people who are not the 'hottest' though? Nothing good, not without a lot of help.

Sex sells of course and that's why despite articles on the likes of Supergrass, REM and one of the most gifted footballers of his generation, Dennis Bergkamp, it was two young women in not very much clothing who adorned the front cover and not any of the boys. It was into this culture that the so-called 'female fronted bands', God help us, arrived and in which they had to attempt to be something other than someone for men to either fear or leer at - or both. It was, and there can be no argument about it, a toxic environment and every review, every article and every photo shoot was cut through by how much 'looked-at-ness' the writer felt they deserved.

However, despite all of this underlying misogyny, the nineties thrust many female artists into the spotlight. Elastica, Sleeper and Echobelly were obviously the biggest names but there were several other bands with female singers or musicians who made a dent in the charts and found a place in the hearts of music fans.

When Tiny Monroe, fronted by the enigmatic N.J, released one of the best singles of the era 'VHF 855V' in 1993 it suggested that here at last we had a band who could rival Suede for a sort of sleazy glamour. N.J's vocals and the thunderously glam racket of the band combined to make it a debut single that deserves to be talked about with the same sort of hushed awe that is normally reserved for 'The Drowners' or 'Supersonic' by Oasis. There would be three more singles and an album over the next three years but with a lack of press coverage and the arrival of lad culture, the writing was on the wall and the band simply disappeared.

It wasn't just Tiny Monroe, there were other female acts who deserved much greater success but who were denied their place in the sun by the arrival of Oasis and the new lads. Jacqui Blake and Carrie Askew, Manic Street Preachers disciples, decided that adoring the boys in the band wasn't enough and so formed their own band, Shampoo and, working with Lawrence from Felt/ Denim, they released a debut single 'Blisters and Bruises' in 1993. Part playground chant, part glam rock stomp, it was a wonderful pop song and contained all of the things that the 'real' music fans who bestow Messiah status on the likes of Cast and Ocean Colour Scene claim to love: guitars, melodies, songs penned by the band, and yet they were, and still are, treated with a level of disdain that suggests that something vital must have been missing. You could spend a long time trying to work out what that is, but I can save you the time: it was a penis. Just that. However, despite the contempt and derision, they still sold a lot of records, scoring a huge hit with 'Trouble' in 1994. They were also genuinely big in Japan.

1993 threw another 'female fronted band' into the mix with Salad. Fronted by former MTV Europe VJ, Marijne Van Der Vlugt, they were responsible for some of the finest singles of the time, with 'Motorbike to Heaven' and 'Drink the Elixir' still floor fillers at any Britpop event even now. But at the height of the scene they managed to release just two albums before, like Tiny Monroe, disappearing. They have recently returned though and released four albums in the last five years.

Although never really seen as part of the Britpop scene, one other band who perfectly illustrate both the quality of music being released by female artists during this period of the nineties and the disdain and discomfort of 'traditional' music fans for them was Huggy Bear. A riot grrrl band, who took their inspiration from the US riot grrrl scene led by the iconic Kathleen Hanna and her band Bikini Kill, they were fiercely political and they refused to be photographed or interviewed by the mainstream press. They caught the attention of the Britpop crowd following an incendiary performance of their song 'Her Jazz' on cult Channel 4 show 'The Word'. They looked and sounded like nobody else at the time and I was hooked. What really cemented their place in my heart though was their response to a report on two American models who called themselves 'The Barbi Twins'; unhappy with the tone of the piece the band started haranguing the host, Terry Christian, before having to be forcibly ejected from the studio.

A lot of people like to tell the tale of seeing Oasis perform 'Supersonic' on the same show and of how it changed their lives. It may have, although I don't know how or why seeing the same sort of faces, playing the same sort of music, could be life changing. But, for me, and I suspect for the other kids like me, seeing Huggy Bear and watching how they challenged the orthodox culture of the time was actually genuinely life changing.

We could go on and on. Dubstar, Kenickie, Republica, Powder, Lush and many other incredible bands all forced their way onto the turntables of the art-school crowd during Britpop, but despite their brilliance and their radicalism they were never given the opportunities that were afforded to the dad rockers.

Chapter 9

Click Off Gone Return

Sleeper

In their twenties Louise Wener and Jon Stewart found themselves in the city that had spawned The Smiths, Joy Division, Factory Records, the Hacienda and so much more. Studying at Manchester University they found themselves drawn together by their creative similarities and after graduating they did what anyone with an ounce of ambition does and moved to London.

Gigs.

Bands.

More gigs.

More bands.

Writing.

Playing.

Getting better.

Finding other people to make things whole.

Here come Diid Osman and Andy Maclure.

Things are beginning to take shape.

Find form.

Louise has brought a bag of records from her childhood and adolescence with her and trapped inside her mind are Boney M, Barbara Dickson, Squeeze, Blondie, Irene Cara, Queen, Madness, The Jam - a mess of influences, a wonderful mess of influences. Jon is more interested in The Pixies and the edgier sounds of what is coming out of America at the start of the nineties. He's casting his net wider than the things he remembers and wants to find new things to get excited by.

What does it sound like when you put two fiercely intelligent, passionate music lovers in a band and throw all of those peculiarities of pop and rock together? Probably not very good nine times out of ten. It would sound like two people trying to be different. It would sound like four people trying too hard. It would sound muddled and confused.

It may have sounded like that for Sleeper at the beginning too. Maybe.

But that mixed-up, muddled-up, shook-up stew of influences and differences, along with some other tensions, created something other than the slop that most other groups would have produced. It produced, without argument, the finest pop group of the nineties.

Yes it did.

It's June 1993 and Indolent Records have grabbed Sleeper, put them in a studio and told them to make music. The 'New Wave of New Wave'[1] is still sort of a thing but, thankfully, Sleeper arrived too late to be lumped in with that. Fortunately, something else is brewing in the kitchen of pop and that something is going to help propel Sleeper to places that bands like them were never meant to get to.

Bands like them.

There were no bands like them in 1993.

Not really.

There very nearly wasn't any band like them, had it not been for a moment of Malcolm McLaren-esque, Machiavellian genius from Louise. Certain that what she and Jon had could be even better, she set about securing a review in the NME for their efforts.

---

1. The scene before Britpop and another music press creation. Bands like Shed Seven, These Animal Men and S*M*A*S*H were NWONW acts who would go on to find chart success during the Britpop era.

Sort of. What she *actually* did was write her own review of her own band and then make it look like it had been culled from the pages of the NME in an effort to persuade Andy Maclure and Diid Osman to join them.

By the time the 'Alice EP' was released in 1993, the pop music that we had always known and loved in Britain had become dominated by a synthetic, fake, over-produced, tinny, dim and dumb gang of boy and girl bands whose only real talent was the ability to rise from a stool on the key change in any given song. The sort of pop music that The Smiths had taken into the mainstream, that Orange Juice had dragged into the charts, that the baggy boys had bundled onto Top of the Pops had, spectacularly, disappeared.

You could apparently either have Boyzone or you could have the American howl of Kurt Cobain.

Neither one was pop music.

Sleeper may well have found something to charm them in Nirvana, Hole, The Pixies and the rest but, in their hearts, it was pop music that they really believed in. Pop music allowed you to reach into the kitchens of suburbia, to touch and influence the lives of other kids just like you, to change the culture - or at least it had the potential to do so when it was done properly.

'Swallow' was the second single from the band and lyrically it was the sound of someone who had not only read but had actually understood Germaine Greer. It was the secret diary of any teenage girl, of every woman. When Morrissey talked about 'The Female Eunuch' that's all he was doing - talking. He didn't really understand it. Here was someone who not only got it but who actually *lived* it. Musically it was what The Breeders would have sounded like if they had come from Gants Hill. Which is a good thing.

What you don't understand is quite how 'other' Louise Wener was in 1993, when she was like a tsunami hitting the world of rock, pop and indie. She was a genuine force, blasting things like sexism, industry expectations and labels out of her path with a wit, verve, guts, guile and style that made her a bona fide icon to thousands of young women, and men, across the country.

When she spoke we listened as here was someone with actual things to say about things that mattered and who said them loudly and without apology. What wasn't to love?

When she said 'We should both go to bed 'til we make each other sore' on 'Delicious', I didn't know what to think, or where to look. All I did know was that even though I wasn't exactly an experienced love maker and I didn't really know what exactly one could do under the covers to make myself, or anyone else, sore, I wanted to find out. This was also the first record that sounded like Sleeper. The influences had faded into the background and into the foreground came their own sound and style.

Click.

Sleeper were about to become more than just a band.

> *'We have a wit and cleverness that other bands could only dream of having.'*
> (Louise Wener, Melody Maker, 13 April 1996)

If Louise had made that remark in 1993 she would have been given a pat on the head, a sympathetic sneer from the journalist and then been dismissed as a 'gobby bird'. In 1993 Sleeper hadn't had any top forty singles and hardly anybody outside my bedroom had ever heard them. By April 1996 though they were a bona fide big deal. No longer a supporting act to the big boys (and they were almost all boys) at the top of the Britpop pyramid but stars in their own right.

The reaction to that comment in 1996 was still a pat on the head along with a sympathetic sneer from almost everyone and instant dismissal though. 'Who does she think she is?' you could hear the blokes who enjoyed wailing 'Wonderwall' at closing time screech.

A female fronting a band at a time when the patronising and ghettoisation of women was tolerated but not accepted.

This was sexism for sure but the real reason for this hostility was something simpler - *jealousy*.

Sleeper were not playing the game the way they were supposed to.

Louise was meant to be pretty.

Or talented.

Not both.

The boys in the band were meant to resent her.

Or tolerate her.

They didn't.

They loved her.

Just like *we* loved her.

Talking like this was the preserve of boys like Liam Gallagher or Martin Rossitter. Confidence like that was the preserve of lads in parkas, not girls.

Bleurgh.

Who did she think she was?

Fortunately for British pop music she knew exactly who she was.

The sneering and the sexism, the lasciviousness and the leering didn't fade with time. Take a look at that 2002 interview Louise did with Ralph Little when, within seconds of the interview beginning, he is happily confessing to having masturbated while thinking of her when he was a teenager. She isn't a fool, she knows that men, particularly teenage boys, do these sorts of things but can you imagine the same thing happening to a male guest? She was there to discuss her career, her music, her writing, to offer opinions and then she is reduced to an object within moments.

'Delicious' was the moment when I joined the story, albeit from the fringes, and as a passive participant in the tale.

A fan.

It is ridiculous to try and pretend that I wasn't a little bit besotted with Louise as after all, I was a boy in his early twenties who didn't know who he was or what he wanted to do with his life. I had had one proper girlfriend and she was now living on the opposite side of the country from me and, most importantly, I had a funny feeling that Louise Wener knew my life better than anyone in any other band did.

I would have loved a girlfriend like her.

But, in all honesty, I was more interested in having a best friend like her.

Someone smart.

Someone confident.

Someone whose coat tails I could hold onto as they dragged me into a life less ordinary.

The fact that 'Delicious' reached number seventy five in the UK charts suggests that I was almost alone in my belief that Sleeper were a band worthy of love and devotion. True it had gone higher than 'Swallow' but only by one place and it looked like that might be enough to consign the band to the footnotes of the story of British pop in the nineties.

A tragedy.

That's what it would have been.

A bloody tragedy.

Enter Dale Winton.

Like every other student and unemployed person in Britain in 1993 I spent my mornings watching 'Supermarket Sweep'. The show saw contestants answer such taxing questions as 'It comes in a container, is full of vitamins, especially if freshly squeezed - what product am I?'. That is a genuine question from the show. It wasn't exactly 'Only Connect'. The host of the show was Dale Winton with his pastel coloured blazers, immaculately coiffed hair, a permanent tan and the sort of high camp that we Britons specialise in.

Winton was, and we have to be honest here, the star of the video for Sleeper's fourth single, 'Inbetweener' and you can decide for yourself whether it was this fact or the brilliance of the record itself that blasted a band who had been lurking around the lower ends of the top 100 into the top twenty. I know what I think.

'Inbetweener' is the moment that Sleeper became a big deal in places that were not in my head.

It's a tale of suburban humdrum existence, wasted opportunities and, most terrifying of all, *settling*. It is a recognisable tale of life in Britain - like a musical version of 'The Royle Family'.

'He's nothing special, she's not too smart...'

Everyone has been in that relationship.

You are together and yet utterly apart.

Tolerating one another.

This isn't a tale of domestic abuse but of the truth of so many relationships, where you feel love but are not in love, where the only passion being felt is for the moments when you are apart and the longing is not for one another but for a Kit-Kat and a box-set.

Inbetweeners who have become forevers.

Get out.

After that came seven more top forty singles, each one the sort of infectious pop song that requires a course of penicillin after you hear them for the first time. Not because you want to be cured, but because you need to be able to function.

Each of them was either a song about love or about ordinary life or a melding of the two. Each of them was clever - too clever for 'Supermarket Sweep'. Each of them was witty and poignant. Each of them was political and personal. You will have your favourite.

You may even have more than one.

You may be one of *those* people who says they are all your favourite.

You are right no matter which it is.

But there is only one correct choice really.

'What Do I Do Now?'

Why?

That's easy - it was hilarious and poignant, sometimes at the same moment. The very best songs always hit you in more than one place. The heart and the gut. The head and the soul. That's exactly what 'What Do I Do Now?' managed.

Somebody once told me that they had done something awful to me. A terrible betrayal.

After they told me what they had done I cried. For days. Something broke. After a few impossible days together, I found myself alone at home. I put on a favourite record and danced around the room.

When the record ended the room was filled with the sound of the crackle and hiss of the run out grooves and the deafening roar of my own tears hitting the floor, and I asked myself, *what do I do now*?

1997 produced a third album and a couple of singles but the time was up for Sleeper and they disappeared from view almost as quickly as they had arrived. It felt like a whimper, a reluctant resignation from the only life they had known or wanted. No Gallagher brothers style falling out, no Damon-esque desire to write operas and discover world music and cartoons - it was just the end of the line.

Off.

New lives.

Families.

Careers.

Writing.

Lecturing.

It was over.

1997 ended...1998 started...then ended...then another new year...a new era...the millennium...history repeating itself...ten years since Britpop...fifteen years...the twentieth anniversary…documentaries about the era…there is Louise telling us all about it…

Gone.

Then a whisper.

And a murmur.

Finally came the confirmation.

Sleeper were reforming for a series of live dates.

I bought a ticket.

Can I be honest with you?

I bought it with hope but not expectation.

It seemed too good to be true.

I was certain that something would happen to leave me disappointed.

This wasn't the usual rock and roll reunion.

There was no greatest hits album to flog on behalf of the record label, which meant that Sleeper were not getting back together just because they wanted to relive the good old days.

They did appear though and it was everything I had hardly dared hope that it would be.

The songs sounded fresh and relevant.

The band looked vibrant and sounded stronger than ever before.

You know what it sounded like?

It sounded like an eraser rubbing out the full stop that had been put on the Sleeper story in 1997.

Since that point there have been two albums of new material ('The Modern Age' and 'This Time Tomorrow') and tours and collaborations with other bands (Jon plays regularly with The Wedding Present). What the future holds is anyone's guess but what the return of Sleeper tells us is that far from being the starting point of what was, cruelly, labelled 'landfill indie' by sneering snoots in the music press, Britpop was a home for people like Wener, who were brash when they needed to be, vulnerable at their core, enviably gifted and who shone so brightly that we can still see them now.

Chapter 10

My Home Too

Echobelly

Sonya Aurora Madan is not, by any stretch of the imagination, your typical pop or rock star. She's so far removed from the typical that she probably can't even be placed on the same cultural continent. She's a genuine original. Just think about the sorts of bands who were making it big in the 90s when she burst onto the music scene – none of them sounded, or looked, like Madan. None of them had lived her experience. She was fiercely intelligent and an all too rare person of colour in the whiter than white world of British indie music.

It would be ridiculous not to acknowledge how significant seeing an Asian woman fronting a guitar band and singing about feminism, abortion and the rest of it was in the early 1990s, especially, I would think, for other young Asian people when only the equally fabulous Cornershop were putting Asian faces into indie kid bedrooms. That's quite a big cultural barrier to be knocking down. It wasn't just Sonya who was a bit 'different' from the indie norms either, as the band also included the openly gay, black Debbie Smith on guitar and a Swedish lead guitarist in the form of Glenn Johansson.

> '*The only thing we had in common was our love of music and the fact that we were all Londoners. (Actually, most Britpop bands came from outside*

*London although a few adopted a mock-cockney
swagger). We were not that easily definable visually
because of our backgrounds, but that ironically, also
made us a perfect example of a multi-cultural capital
city melting pot.'*

(Glenn Johansson, 2017)

The 'Bellyache' EP was the band's calling card. It arrived late in
1993 just a few months before Britpop became a 'thing'. Earlier
in the year, Blur had released 'Modern Life is Rubbish' and
Suede were already a 'big deal' but nobody knew what an Oasis
was or that Pulp even existed. Even the 'Shagging in the Streets'
EP which was the calling card of the New Wave of New Wave
(Britpop's punkier older brother) wasn't released until the next
year. So this release was a crucial moment in the history of a
major popular culture movement.

I bought my copy from Stereo One in Paisley. Situated behind
Gilmour Street train station, this was a safe haven for me during
my years studying at the university there. I spent hours browsing
the shelves and deposited a large chunk of my student loans in
the cash register. I bought my first Pulp record there ('Lipgloss'),
'Stay Together' by Suede on 12", 'For the Dead' by Gene, 'Lady
Love Your Cunt' by S*M*A*S*H, 'Speeed King' by These Animal
Men and too many others to mention.

The title track was a clear indication that this was not a frivolous
band. It's a dark and deeply intimate portrait of love gone wrong,
with very real consequences. 'It's more than a bellyache, there's
something alive in here'.

It opens with a Bo Diddley riff that was reworked in a style
reminiscent of 'How Soon is Now' by The Smiths. That, and the
lyrical content, saw lots of comparisons with those Mancunian
masters of mope and misery being drawn by lazy journalists. The
truth was much more complicated. Echobelly were a rare beast, a

band that arrived fully formed and with their own sound. It really wasn't easy to say who, if anyone, they reminded you of.

That said, the second track on the EP, 'Sleeping Hitler', does doff its cap to Morrissey with the line: 'I wish I was blindly loved' which is similar to 'I would sooner be just blindly loved' from the Morrissey song 'The Harsh Truth of the Camera Eye' from his 1991 album 'Kill Uncle'. Legend has it that the Pope of Mope himself took quite the shine to Echobelly, so much so that he turned up at the home of Sonya.

> *'It's true, he did show up one day. He was very friendly and the cat liked him as well which was a good sign for us. Slightly embarrassing though since the cat was called Morrissey! He asked what the cat was called and we were put on the spot but managed to make something up. He said he really liked the band and was particularly impressed by some of Sonya's song titles. He came to see us play a few times and always came backstage after the show for a chat. The Smiths were one of the reasons why I decided to move from Sweden to London. I was a huge fan but I don't think Sonya was that aware of them at the time. I will always have a huge respect for Morrissey.'*
>
> (Glenn Johansson, 2017)

The closing track of the EP is 'I Don't Belong Here' which might, just might, be a subtle rebuke for the line in 'Bengali in Platforms' from 'Viva Hate' where Morrissey sings: 'Shelve your Western plans, life is hard enough when you belong here'. It's safe, I think, to assume that given the proximity to this song and Morrissey's 'Flying the flag… flirting with disaster' debacle the year before its release, both events were probably linked.

The band's debut album, 'Everyone's Got One' arrived in the summer of 1994, shortly before 'Definitely Maybe' and, despite a lukewarm response from some of the music papers, it reached number eight in the charts. There were towering pop anthems like 'I Can't Imagine The World Without Me', which could make claim for the top spot in any list of singles released during that era, with its rolling, pounding, drilling drums and the aural treat of Madan yelling 'me, me, me, me, me'. There's also the sheer craft of the melody that was delivered by Glenn Johansson. It's a terrific pop single.

There is one moment in the album that elevates the band, from being just a band to being a band worthy of your love. That moment is 'Insomniac' which in a better world would have been number one on release and would be number one still. It's perfect. In every respect.

Lyrically the song deals with one of the dominant features of that time in British popular culture: cocaine. Let there be no doubt that Britain in the mid 1990s was buried under an avalanche of white powder. Its 'influence' can be heard all over certain records from that time, most obviously 'Be Here Now' by Oasis and 'The Second Coming' by fellow Mancs, The Stone Roses. Bombastic. Over produced. Dull. Occasional flashes of the old magic. That's the truth of those records, and others, and it's also true of the musicians responsible. 'Whatever turned you on, you put it up your nose dear' sings Sonya while Glenn and the gang provide a musical backdrop that is so clean, so crisp and so free from the influence of charlie that it ranks as the toppermost of the pops for many connoisseurs of Britpop.

'I remember it as a really vibrant time, not only for music but for British culture in general. There was a real sense of confidence and pride in the musical past. There were many highlights, our first sold out

headline tour, touring with REM, private planes and meeting various artists that you admired but most of it is a bit of a blur (not the band) due to the hedonistic lifestyle that accompanied those times.'

(Glenn Johansson, 2017)

In chart terms Echobelly peaked in 1995 when their second album, 'On', spawned a couple of top thirty singles and reached number four. By the time a third album, 'Lustra', arrived the Britpop juggernaut was already beginning to slow down. The era of dad rock had begun, the rot had set in, and nobody wanted to hear the sort of dark, brooding, thoughtful and intelligent pop music that they were making. People are stupid. But it wasn't the end of the band as Glenn and Sonya have continued to write, record and perform and have released a further three albums.

That they have a body of work that stands beside the very best of the era isn't up for debate, but their importance stretches beyond just the music. Seeing Sonya in that Union Flag T-shirt with 'My country too' scrawled across it helped young people like me to think more carefully about the darker side of 'Cool Britannia' and ask where the black and brown voices were? Where was the line between patriotism and nationalism? Was 'Yanks go Home' really the sort of thing I wanted to be saying or thinking? Pop music should be fun and many of its finest moments are meaningless and throwaway, but it still needs to say *something*, at least every once in a while, otherwise it has no real value. Echobelly were saying something, but I wonder who was listening?

Chapter 11

Get Our Pictures In The Papers

For every band who smashed into the charts and onto the front pages of the tabloid press there were two or three others that nobody outside of the scene ever heard or heard of. Thurman, Mantaray and The Weekenders are three examples of what was going on away from the gaze of the mainstream media.

Outside the big hitters, the world of Britpop was filled with bands who burned bright then faded away; dozens of magnesium flash acts who appeared, and disappeared, without anyone really noticing. For many people nowadays, the label of Britpop means dad rock, trad rock and revivalist acts like Ocean Colour Scene, Cast and post-Wildwood Weller. That isn't the real story of the era though, it's just the fall out of the way in which Oasis came to dominate the cultural landscape thanks to their antics and constant media presence. For the kids on the street it wasn't the prospect of another song that sounded a bit like Oasis that was exciting, it was the prospect of discovering something new and a bit peculiar.

If Britpop was about anything it was about outsiders, even if too many people see it as some sort of Mod revival, a tourist shop celebration of Britishness or a chance to do some live action role play, like people at Star Trek conventions but with a bucket hat replacing Kirk's uniform or Spock's ears. After the initial rejection of grunge, the Brit in Britpop became less and less important and the pop emerged as the key thing.

Seeing people like me on Top of the Pops was a thrill and people like me were not people like Noel and Liam, they were something different.

The way in which Oasis came to control the narrative around the time and exert a faintly toxic influence on indie music can still be felt today, almost three decades later. They managed to squeeze out the fey girls and boys, cut off the oxygen supply for the eccentric and plain weird and replace them with a legion of macho, beer soaked über lads who thought it was enough to imitate and not create.

Some of the less blokey bands at the time still managed to find a route to the mainstream though with Gene, Shampoo, Cornershop and Saint Etienne all enjoying chart success and building loyal followings while older bands like James and The Charlatans also managed to ride the Britpop wave and find a whole new audience.

By the time we reached 1996 it was obvious that Britpop had divided into two tribes. The new lads who embraced Loaded and took the lyrics of 'Cigarettes and Alcohol' as an instruction manual and the art school crowd, who embraced the sexual ambiguity of Suede, the performance art of David Devant and His Spirit Wife and the top of the fops delights of Jarvis Cocker. This wasn't a Mods vs rockers division though and people on both sides could still enjoy the music each was producing, even if it was clear that they were most definitely two different tribes.

The most interesting and exciting bands were obviously the ones in the latter camp (and they usually were camp) who liked to dress up, bear their souls and break our hearts. Few achieved any real success and some barely managed to release any music but for people like me, they are a vital, integral part of the story of Britpop.

Thurman, in many ways, were the perfect Britpop band and yet, outside of the most devout followers of the scene, nobody knows who they were.

Britpop is a scene that is often derided by the media. It's dismissed on the dual grounds of being frivolous and lacking 'authenticity'. Quite why anyone would want anything from pop music other than frivolity and why everything needs to be authentic is beyond me. When you're dancing at the disco, bumper to bumper, the only thing you are interested in is having a good time - not questioning whether or not the singer is a genuine cockney or if the song is a commentary on Marxist dialectic. Maybe that's just me though.

NICK KENNY (SINGER, THURMAN) '*It was a sunny time. I've got really fond memories of going to Blow Up, meeting some really beautiful people and there being so many gigs to go to. I just loved travelling to Camden and meeting people, going shopping in Miss Selfridge for shirts and make up, then just hanging out with people at gigs. A happy time really and it was very free of politics. The media LOVED it too. If they try to tell you otherwise now they are fucking liars.*'

Thurman were a band with magpie eyes, who wore their influences, and their hearts, on their sleeves, utterly unafraid to let the world know who they loved, who they were listening to and who they wanted to be.

NK '*Our influences at that time were The Who, Bowie, The Kinks and Bolan. I think we did wear our influences on our sleeves, certainly as much as any other band at that time did, but there was one particular song we recorded, 'Loaded', which was a bona fide steal! When we were recording our album, 'Lux', we would be listening to our contemporaries and spotting the steals they were doing and we tried to out-steal them. It might not have been a great idea as the press used it as a stick to beat us with.*'

One of the reasons Thurman invoked the wrath of certain journalists at the time was because they hadn't always been mod/glam Britpoppers. In fact they had previously been a metal band called 2 Die 4. I know, right. The horror. Imagine playing different music and having changing tastes. The truth is, of course, that like all of us, people in bands change.

NK '*Oh the indie press really hated us for it. There was a massive snobbery that came from the NME and Melody Maker towards rock or metal bands at the time. In fact, there still is with many 'alternative journalists'. Me and my brother Simon described ourselves as rock and roll culture junkies from a very early age.*

When we first got into music, we were listening to The Cramps, Iggy Pop, Bowie, Elvis, a lot of cool English rockabilly music that was around in the '80s, Sputnik, The Clash. It was a journey of musical discoveries. And what we listened to would reflect in the music our band would play. By the time we got halfway through secondary school we were discovering Van Halen, AC/DC, Mötley Crüe, and all the rest, on our musical journey. Our band reflected our current record collection, and once I'd turned fifteen, we'd been signed up to a major record label in America. They flew us out to Los Angeles to make the record, I said bye bye school, and we had the time of our lives! I wasn't singing then, just playing guitar. We were on MTV, travelled the world, lived the rock and roll life, and after a couple of years, it was clear that we weren't gonna get a chance to make another record with that band, so it ended.

The singer Andy Shaw went back home to Liverpool. That left me, my brother and Diz in a rehearsal room playing records, and making music. While 2 Die 4 was born out of our disdain for English music at that time, Thurman was a bit of a reaction to our American experience, and a rediscovery of cool 60s pop culture. And finally, there were some good bands emerging, like Suede, Blur, PJ Harvey and Pulp. We formed a record label with our management... and off we went!'

Out went the hair licks and long hair of 2 Die 4 and in came the mop tops and glam riffs of Thurman. I first heard them in 1994 on the Fierce Panda compilation 'Return to Splendour'[1] with a song called 'This Way', which was followed by a single that was so Britpop it could have been made the national anthem for the independent state of Britpopia. That single was 'English Tea'. Urging its listeners to have a cuppa, talk about the weather, read the papers and do it all on a luvverly day.

'Talk to Myself' was the next single to see the light before the release of their first and, sadly, only album 'Lux', the following year. It sounds a lot like 'Modern Life is Rubbish' era Blur. It also sounds a lot like The Kinks. This was just one of the great things about Thurman: they were a jukebox of British pop influences that all came together to form a sound that was distinctly their own 'Lux' arrived in 1995 and with any sort of support at all it would have been massive. Sam Upton at Select magazine was a near lone voice in offering a fair and positive review of the album, awarding it four stars out of five. On the subject of influences vs plagiarism he had this to say: *'But as most bands today aren't renowned for their high moral stance on plagiarism, Thurman at least are in good company.'* [2] When one thinks of the pilfering by Elastica, Menswe@r and The Verve, to name just three, it's clear that there was an agenda at work by certain journalists who had decided that Thurman and their rock band past didn't pass the 'authenticity' test.

The album kicks off with a proper glam stomper in the shape of 'She's a Man'. It's so steeped in Bowie and Bolan boogie that it's difficult not to want to dig out your mum's old platform boots and strut your way around the bedroom singing into a hairbrush. It sounds dumb and young, just like all the best pop songs should. A year earlier Morrissey had released his own glam rock record 'Your Arsenal' which had included a direct rip off of the T-Rex classic 'Ride a White Swan' in the single 'Certain People I Know'. Given

---

1. The EP, released in December 1994, also featured The Bluetones.
2. Select, October 1995

the presence of rockabilly legend Boz Boorer from The Polecats and well-known music obsessive Alain Whyte in the band, that wasn't all that surprising. But while that track was welcomed as funny old Mozzer doffing his cap to a hero, Thurman's 'Loaded' was greeted with a lot of sniffing and harrumphing.

NK '*We'd been tagged early on as a mod band, and we were pretty keen to show our glam influences on the album.*'

Before 'She's a Man' was released the band let loose the jaunty 'Famous' as their third single. It's a thousand times better than 'Sunday Sunday' by Blur but, again, it failed to bring the band to a wider audience or to win over the press.

Despite not receiving the success or recognition they deserved, life in Thurman during this era was still more exciting and glamorous than one might suspect.

NK '*I'd say one of the highlights was going over to Japan for a tour. As soon as we landed, we had loads of girls following us everywhere we went. I remember going through passport control, and seeing a group of glammed up girls waving and crying, and I thought there must be someone famous behind me, but it soon became clear they were there for us!*

They were amazing fans, who would send lovely letters, and make prints for us, or shirts, or food... really dear people. So polite too. By contrast, a low point was our van breaking down outside Edinburgh castle after a gig. It was snowing, and the sliding side door wouldn't fully close... we were covered in sweat, freezing cold, unable to move and with an eight hour journey ahead of us to get home.'

The advantage Thurman had with a Japanese audience was that they were judging the band on the music and not on the attitudes of the music weeklies in dear old Blighty.

NK '*I think we just felt that we had got as far as we were gonna get with it. The press were pretty tough on us, and I remember they would just lie about things. There was one live review they did of us in Oxford. They wrote that even in our hometown, there was hardly anyone attending the show. In fact, we had sold it out. They just fucking hated us. Agendas were made, and I guess we just didn't have enough cocaine to grease the palms of certain hands.*'

Mantaray were, like Thurman, a band who managed to capture the hearts of audiences and secure a record deal but didn't quite make the step from contenders to stars. They were one of the most exciting live bands of the era and were arguably the most Mod of any of the groups who emerged.

CHRIS LATTIMER (singer, Mantaray) '*It's funny looking back on it, everyone wants to be in a band. We wanted to make records. We got the chance to do that. It was exciting. We were doing the things that the people we respected were doing. If it wasn't exciting, who would want anything to do with it? When we started it was that shoegaze scene, I'm astonished that anyone survived seeing us when you think about what those bands were like!*'

Before Britpop was a thing, Mantaray were already doing their own thing, marking their own territory. Chris and Dave (Standen) had been in a band together since they were eleven years old. What Britpop offered them wasn't the inspiration to start a band but a chance for the band they already had to be heard.

CL '*We probably appeared a bit cartoony in comparison to some of the other bands at the time we first started playing in London. We were always Mods, it was important to us to dress well...it was important too that the people on the stage looked good. We had a* *public persona of being a bit arrogant, but it was for fun. Behind the scenes we were as nice as pie.'*

In February 1994 the indie label Fierce Panda released an EP called 'Shagging in the Streets' that featured tracks from S*M*A*S*H, Blessed Ethel, Done Lying Down, Action Painting! and speed kings These Animal Men, alongside a demo track by Mantaray called 'Sad'.

S*M*A*S*H and These Animal Men were already attracting a fair bit of attention from the press, S*M*A*S*H because they were a bit like the Manic Street Preachers, albeit with slightly less poetry, and These Animal Men because they came from Brighton and were consuming industrial quantities of amphetamine, allegedly.

'Sad' was the outstanding track on the EP. It sounded like The Jam and The Clash and The Television Personalities and all sorts of other classic English power pop. It also had a bit of swearing and everyone loves a bit of swearing in a pop song, it adds a certain something to a car journey home with your dad when you pop your mix-tape into the cassette deck.

In Chris Latter, Mantaray had a singer who was unafraid to be a showman, something that very definitely set them apart from the likes of Chapterhouse and Swervedriver at the start of the nineties but, more importantly, he was also a writer who was happy to tackle serious issues without ever sounding worthy. When their debut album, 'Some Pop' arrived, it included songs whose titles alone were enough to set them apart and put them in a different lane to the lad rockers - 'Closet Hetero', 'When You Say Yes' and 'If You Were a Girl' were a world away from certain big chart hits from other Britpop acts.

Finding themselves on 'Shagging in the Streets' could have been down to being in the right place, at the right time and in front of the right people but my hope is that it happened the way that Chris remembers it.

CL *'I don't remember much but I do remember at those early gigs I was wearing desert boots, white Levi's, a target t-shirt and a white Levi cord jacket. If you want to get a record out, that's the way I did it. That Mod thing was important to me, it was like a uniform. I spent every last penny I had buying a Rickenbacker guitar before I was even in a band because I knew nothing could happen without a Rickenbacker.'*

The Weekenders were Paul Tunkin[3] on vocals, James Hender on guitar, Chris Remington on bass and Steve Smith on drums. They sounded like *London*. Specifically they sounded like London in 1994: soaked in Kinks melodies, drenched in the fury of The Jam and The Buzzcocks, bathed in the glories of England's pop past but gearing up to be the sound of England's present and maybe future too.

Their debut single was a mail order slab/stab of the most quintessentially British of Britpop. 'All Grown Up' backed with 'Househusband'. They sounded like they may have been recorded in my front room and were raw, rough around the edges and all the better for it. To be honest it doesn't actually matter all that much what The Weekenders sounded like, there were more important things to consider about bands at this point like did they come from London? Were they Mods? Did the singer have a girlfriend who was in Elastica? Big picture stuff.

While this first single wasn't exactly the stuff of legend, musically speaking as nobody now talks about it in hushed, reverential tones and my copy would probably fetch about 75 pence on eBay, their next single was genuinely brilliant.

---

3. Paul was the tour DJ on Blur's 'Parklife' tour and the main man at the legendary club Blow Up! Paul still runs Blow Up!, and the label of the same name.

'Seems You Missed Sunday' was a hymn to staying out all night, taking loads of drugs and then crashing out for 24 hours. Simple stuff but stuff that when set to a cracking, crackling, melody can make the hairs on the back of your balls stand on end.

There was one more single which, for its title alone, deserves to still be number one in the charts: '*Inelegantly Wasted in Papa's Penthouse Pad in Belgravia*'. Told you. Number one title. That was it. All over for The Weekenders. A mini album[4] emerged that compiled all of the singles but a proper album never emerged which, I think, is a real shame because few other bands captured the Britpop 'scene' better than The Weekenders.

They were fun, they were energetic, they had the right clobber and, while I was cleaning the toilets of the local McDonald's, they were living the dream.

---

4. 'That Was Now But This Is Then', 1995.

Chapter 12

Are You Happy Now?

The untold story of Lick

'Oh, don't I look beautiful?'

(Stargazer)

'We're a mixture of hard and soft, masculine and feminine, which is a healthier outlook than being one or the other.'

(Gary Cosby, NME, 3/6/1995)

You don't even know that your favourite band of all time is Lick.

How could you?

You blinked and missed them.

As the press flung one gang of pretenders after another in your face between 1993 and 1997 you missed the one gang who really understood The Pretenders and all the other glories of post-punk and New Wave and who really got the fact that nothing, absolutely nothing, matters more than looking good.

Tragedy.

As I lay in a lost and lonely part of town, in a world of tears I slowly drowned and I really couldn't make it on my own, I should have been holding onto Lick.

Holding them.

Loving them.

Now they're gone and I don't know if I should go on.

Tragedy.

'Last night we had a very rare experience in the shape of a gigantic shooting star. It crossed the sky about a quarter-past 10 o'clock and lit up the country for miles around with a bright green flare, and then faded away to a pink colour. It lasted for several seconds. Several people rushed out of their homes thinking they were in the midst of huge flames. Then about two minutes after the illumination died away there came a rumbling in the heavens which gradually became louder until it was like heavy thunder. The sound travelled the same course as the star.'
(Mr E.T. Easton, Rockhampton, 4/8/1903)

Rockhampton is a city in Queensland, Australia. It is an industrial and agricultural centre. Other than the sighting of a meteor in 1903 there was little of note about the place.

Then the Cosby family had a little baby boy and they called him Gary.

Poor Gary. He knew that he wasn't like the other people in Rockhampton. He had a funny feeling that he wasn't like other people full stop. No matter where they were from. He couldn't be sure about that though, because he hadn't ever been anywhere else. It was just a feeling.

GARY COSBY *'I seriously doubt I would have survived into adulthood there. No, I think I would have been run out of town as soon as I discovered the make-up counter at Coles. Fortunately, I didn't have to hitch a ride, my parents moved us to the Western suburbs of Sydney when I was 13.'*

In Sydney a whole new world was presented to Gary and it was one he instantly understood was the one he was meant to be in - not the one where trains rumble down the centre of the street or where people boast about a meteor sighting from the turn of the century. No, Gary wanted to *be* the meteorite. He wanted to be the sound that travelled the same course as the star and also be the star, all at the same time.

GC 'I would jump on the train and hang out at import record stores in the city, fingering albums by my favourite British artists, imagining myself on the covers. We used to get NME, Melody Maker and Sounds. They were my bibles. London was definitely on my radar from an early age.'

We've all been there of course, thumbing our way through the racks of records, staring at our favourite pop stars and daydreaming of life as a star, but Gary knew that he could actually do it, that it didn't have to be just a daydream.

GC 'At nine years old I wanted to be Suzi Quatro. I was obsessed. I wasn't the only one: Debbie from Echobelly cites her musical epiphany as seeing 'Can The Can' on Top of the Pops. Ha! I wish I'd known that when I was forming a band. Debbie would have looked great in Lick. It was pretty much 'Can The Can' for me until Deborah Harry and Chrissie Hynde came along. It was The Pretenders' first album that made me want to be in a band. Sydney had an incredible music scene in the eighties. My musical background is quite schizoid though, one minute I was a teeny rocker and the next it was all makeup and Duran Duran. I loved punk too - that didn't arrive in Australia until about 1980! I loved 'New Wave' bands as well. I guess I was really trying to find... me.'

I don't trust people who don't like punk and new wave and pop and everything else that pop music has spewed out since Elvis donned his blue suede shoes. That awful, ludicrous, snobbishness of only enjoying music if it fits within some ridiculously narrow *weltanschauung* makes me feel suspicious.

Do you remember that time when you shared a flat with Chrissie Amphlett from The Divinyls? You do. You must do. How you listened to 'I Touch Myself' over and over? You don't? Hmmm. Maybe it was just little Gary. Except he wasn't so little by that point. He was all grown up and one day Chrissie spotted a poster on his wall and said 'Why don't you stop worshipping and do it yourself?' That's a good question, right?

GC '*Within a year, aged twenty two, I'd saved enough to jump on a plane and follow my dream of making it in the music biz in the UK. That's pretty fierce, right?'*

Yes. It is. It's properly fierce.

GC '*I arrived in London and I swear I thought I was going to die, it was so cold. I wasn't alone though. I was with my first boyfriend, a writer. We left immediately, caught the first train to Italy, then lived out the winter on Crete, which is where I knuckled down and started writing songs, dreaming of a sunny London. By the Spring though we were back and squatting in the East End. I got a job at Camden Markets and that's where in the early 90s I first noticed a scene - of sorts - emerging. That scene became Britpop. I wanted in. At the time though I was mainly hanging out on London's gay scene and I just couldn't find anyone like me. I remember I even chatted up Jimmy Somerville - that's how desperate I was - he was having none of it. So I placed an ad in Melody Maker and the first person to respond was Simon Moore (guitarist in Lick). He was such a lovely quiet guy, totally happy just playing his guitar and recording stuff on his 4-track in his bedroom. He looked great. I thought: 'You're coming with me!'. It took ages though before we got an actual band together. For a long time we continued to record and write songs. By the time Britpop came along we were ready to take that step. Enter Andy Stone (drummer) and Simon Walker (bass) - the sweetest guys. I was like their mother though. In fact I was a complete bitch. We rehearsed until our fingers bled. We had to be great - there were so many bands - venues around London were spoilt for choice. Getting a decent gig was like winning the lottery. But we stood out. From day one we stood out. I had no doubt in my mind that we were special.'*

Squatting, Camden, ads in the Melody Maker, Jimmy Somerville, it is from such fertile soil that truly great bands are spawned.

Lick arrived in 1994 and within a few months GLR Radio were playing the demo of 'Stand Up'. That song would eventually become their second single (following the limited edition release of 'Come'/'Shirtlifter' and 'Filming') and it captures so many of the things that make Lick great. A fabulous chorus, riffs that shake you out of your boots, a melody that makes you feel alive and a vocal that seems to have been produced in a Britpop 'Weird Science' lab with a touch of Brett Anderson, a hint of John Lydon and a teeny weeny drop of Simon Le Bon.

GC 'Suddenly we found ourselves playing a gig with Menswe@r that attracted every label in London. I remember that gig very clearly. Menswe@r were terrified. And they weren't happy about going on after us. But, hey, they got that Melody Maker cover. Warner flew in Seymour Stein to see us the following week. We signed to WEA in December. That's crazy, but, you know, I'd been waiting since I was nine years old. I wasn't going to pass that up. No matter how uncool it was to sign direct to a major [Note: Britpop rule No.1 is NEVER sign to a major as NME and Melody Maker will hate you for it]'

Ah.

Seymour Stein.

Here is a quick reminder of why that is a big deal.

Madonna, The Pretenders, Wham, The Ramones, Talking Heads. Stein is a legend. He's like Simon Cowell, but with taste and a genuine understanding of and passion for pop music. So, not like Cowell in any way but I wanted to take a cheap shot at him, and I'm not sorry.

In December of 1994 this is what Stein had to say about Lick:

'Really glad I mustered up the strength to overcome jet-lag and see Lick on Saturday night. Once they were on stage I forgot that I was tired, couldn't get the music out of my head and was up until well past 3 a.m - please DO NOT LOSE THIS DEAL.'

Gary is right of course, the music press don't like people to be successful, unless it is on their terms. Those terms are: we choose who we like, we tell everyone else who to like, we claim all the credit for your success and then ride on your coat tails as a consequence. Signing directly to a major without the press playing any part in it does not meet those criteria.

Good.

That indier than thou attitude so beloved of London hipsters and Glasgow scenesters is bullshit. If you are in a band you should want to be the best band in the world and have your music heard by as many people as possible. The idea that you would want to skulk around in the shadows of some dive bar in Camden or on the Byers Road is just the worst sort of muso snobbery. I want my pop stars to be stars. I want them to sign autographs and be big in Japan or some other far flung exotic place - basically I want my bands to be able to tell me these two stories:

GC 'I can remember the exact moment I was first asked to sign autographs. It was in York. Three girls were waiting outside the venue with our first single - a limited vinyl edition of 'Come'. They were so excited. It was surreal: it was me, back in Sydney, waiting outside The Sebel Townhouse for The Pretenders, Joan Jett, Suzi Quatro. But what was even more amazing was that I'd

131

got my band signed to the same label as that very first Pretenders album. Not by design. They just happened to be the ones who wanted us. I still have those singles of course, they are precious to me. It was actually early in 1996 that we were invited to play in Bangkok of all places. We hopped off the plane and it was like we were already famous. Screaming fans at the airport, waiting for us in the hotel. We had fans in the UK too, but this was at another level. Britpop was huge there, with Suede, The Manic Street Preachers, Shed Seven (who were megastars) all playing to larger audiences than they did here in the UK. Our singles were played on the radio. Our headline show to 5,000 people went out live on TV. We arrived back in the UK in the middle of winter, back on the tube and back to work on our album.'

Britpop is often criticised for being too white, too straight, too laddish and too backwards looking. In some ways those criticisms are fair, but only in some ways. There were people of colour on the scene, there were softer sides to it and there were people looking forward and not just trying to regurgitate the Beatles' back catalogue. There were gay faces and voices to be heard of course: Debbie from Echobelly and Martin Rossiter from Gene would be the most obvious. Controversially Brett Anderson once claimed to be a 'bi-sexual man who has never had a homosexual experience.'

GC 'That 'I'm a bisexual man who has never had a homosexual experience' quote narked me at the time. I can tell you now, none of my gay friends fancied Brett Anderson! I certainly didn't, I had my eye on the drummer in Elastica - my favourite band from that era. I did go to see Suede once though, in Brixton. I had to. There were comparisons. I went to see what all the ridiculous fuss was about. Half a song in I thought: 'Shit. How am I going to compete with that?' There was absolutely no competition being flamingly gay though. There were probably others in bands at the time, but, perhaps wisely, they kept it quiet. It was a different time, you see. It wasn't a great time to be gay and trying to make it in a band. It wasn't a great time to be gay full stop. The community was still recovering from all that eighties AIDS hysteria in the media. And there was still no effective treatment for HIV - that didn't come until around 1996 when Britpop was over. But something actually amazing happened within the gay scene at the same time as Britpop. It fractured. Prior to then, it was pretty much tops-off, muscle Mary dance clubs and leather bars. Suddenly you had clubs like Popstarz, Vaseline and Marvellous popping up and skinny gay guys like me started appearing out of nowhere. I remember thinking 'Hang on a minute, I thought I was the only indie gay!'. That's what, in effect, our single 'Stand Up' was about. It was a call to arms. I originally wanted the video to be full of misfits storming the streets of London. The band and label opted for a performance vid instead. I was outvoted. Ah, well, you know, you can't control everything!'

I can remember visiting Popstarz during that same period and it makes me feel warm and fuzzy to think that I might have been strutting what little stuff I've got on the floor alongside Gary.

There isn't a lot of Lick to *lick*. There was the debut single 'Come' and its double a-side 'Shirtlifter', after which came 'Filming', which was all sorts of wonderful - bouncy, anthemic, heartfelt, punky, spiky and generally ace. Then a final, glam stomper of a single with 'My Summer 31' and then it was all over before it had even properly started.

GC *'After our singles failed to get even C-listed, and the A&R team who signed us left the label, Warner, as a last-ditch attempt, dumped us on a fledgling talent coordinator, Jonathan Dickins (who now manages Adele). Poor guy, he really didn't know what to do with us. He didn't sign us, why would he care? The writing* *was on the wall. The band wasn't getting on. It was awful, so less than two years after we'd formed the other members decided they'd had enough. I felt really bad about the tour we advertised and cancelled. We were gaining fans all the time through coverage in Fanzines and word of mouth. But everyone else felt it just wasn't going to work out for Lick.'* remembers Gary today. As he describes it, you get the feeling that even though it was all a long time ago and he has very definitely moved on, he still feels that there is unfinished business.

He is right, there *is* unfinished business. There is a Lick album. Twelve songs that showcase just how brilliant a band they were and how wonderful Gary was as a writer, singer and pop star.

GC *'I have the album, of course. I think because it came at the very end of Britpop, I really thought that its time had come and gone. But with the resurgence in interest in Britpop, Warner might release it eventually. Who knows? It's a good album.'*

He is wrong, it isn't a good album. It's a *great* album. It is one of those albums that reminds you why you care about pop music the way that you do. It sounds like a Britpop record and at the same time it sounds utterly and absolutely fresh. It wears its heart and its influences on its sleeve and in its grooves but manages to sound only like Lick.

When Mr Easton of Rockhampton described that meteorite back in 1903 he said that it '*lit up the country for miles around with a bright green flare, and then faded away to a pink colour.'* Lick were just like that meteorite, they burned bright, they burned fierce, people saw it, people remember it and, yes, they have faded away but I have a feeling that there might be one last burst to come.

Chapter 13

Here Lies Unfenced Existence

Soda

The shimmer and the shine.

The stars and the starlets.

The sex and the drugs.

The rock and the roll.

Triumph.

That's what we think of when we imagine the life of a rock 'n' roll band - a series of never ending highs along the lines of: form a band, write a song, play a gig, play another gig, write another song, a better song, play another gig to a bigger crowd, get signed, record a single, play some more gigs, release the single, hear the single on the radio, play a gig to an even bigger crowd, record an album, release the album, it's a hit, another gig, another single, another album.

The truth is that for every intoxicating high, for every band who 'make it', for every rags to riches story, there are other stories of missed opportunities, bad luck, misfortune and tragedy.

Soda were a band who captured both sides of the story.

Wondrous highs and bitter lows.

Let's start at the very beginning, which is always a very good place to start.

I had the chance to chat with drummer Carl Lonsdale about the Soda story and twenty years on from the band's premature demise he has shared his thoughts and memories about what unfolded at that time. It's quite the story.

Mind Garden had their origins in Hull in the early nineties. Playing regularly, they built up a loyal local following and were favourites at the city's legendary Adelphi Club. Like all good bands, the line-up was fluid until things felt 'right' and when that happened, Mind Garden were consigned to the dustbin of history and Soda was born at the beginning of 1994. Even before that, the original group had enjoyed some success supporting the likes of Kingmaker, Salad, Kinky Machine, Paris Angels and some chancers from Manchester called Oasis. I wonder what happened to them?

A self-funded single, 'Slave to the Fashion Page', made its way into the hands of the lads from Shed Seven, who asked the band to support them on tour.

CARL LONSDALE (DRUMS) '*We caught the eye of Shed Seven's management at one of these gigs who signed us after putting us in Fairview Studios to record some new Demos. The early 1990s was such a great time for music and bands so we were obviously listening to a lot similar stuff back then. John Peel played a big part in most of our lives, so we were listening to Bands like The Charlatans, The Fall, Loop, Ride, Inspiral Carpets, Blur, Happy Mondays, The La's... but we also liked a lot of 60s stuff like Soft Machine, Yes, The Who and American bands like the Stooges and MC5. Liam, our bass player, introduced us to a lot of good stuff when he joined the band in early 1994, bands like Mantaray and The Flamingos and I seem to remember Liam playing us singles by Shed 7 and Elastica - the first time we had heard them.*'

By 1995 there was a *lot* of buzz around Soda. More than buzz, *noise*. They were a big deal who didn't have a deal. Five lads from the North - Ocean Reid on vocals, Liam Maloy on bass, Mike Milner on guitar, Chris Charlton on rhythm guitar and Carl Lonsdale on drums.

The proof of that is highlighted by the fact that by this time they were supporting the big deals down in London, so that the likes of Supergrass, The Bluetones and Blur had all followed Soda on stage.

What was it like to be right at the very heart of a music scene that was in the midst of dominating an entire country, wooing an entire generation and setting the template for future guitar music in a way that few others have?

CL 'These were heady times, there was so much going on. Is it just me or was the weather always good? I was in a band with my mates. Imagine it, we were just five lads from Hull stood outside the Dublin Castle in London and we've just said 'Hello' to Jarvis Cocker, and then somebody from Elastica is just walking in! We were buzzing because every record label in the country wanted to sign us at that point.

We landed smack bang into the middle of this whirlwind in mid 1995. We also did some more one offs with The Longpigs, Pere Ubu, Cast and Lick and then full UK tours with Mansun and Shed 7. We have mostly happy memories about those early shows - we were honoured to play with a lot of these bands, although we didn't bow down to them; we knew we were good too. There were a few bands along the way that enjoyed being difficult with us, but that's hardly worth a mention...'

When the time came to head into the studio to record, the label presented two producers with a fairly prestigious pedigree - Langer and Winstanley. These chaps had worked with Morrissey on 'Kill Uncle', Madness, Teardrop Explodes, Dexys Midnight Runners, Elvis Costello and the Attractions, Lloyd Cole and the Commotions and others. But was it a bit intimidating to work with people who had worked with that little gang of British pop legends?

137

CL 'We were pretty nonplussed when we heard Langer and Winstanley were going to do the album! Not that we didn't know who they were, or their pedigree, it was kind of like that's who had been chosen to do the album. We kind of had a raw side to us, a bit of an edgier sound with the guitars (which came from listening to punk bands as well as bands like Elastica and Wire) so we were wondering what they would bring to the table.

We recorded our first single 'The Young Own the Town' at Townhouse Studios in Sept 95 with Paul Corket who was doing Strangelove's stuff at the time, then we switched over to Westside Studios with Clive and Alan to record our second single 'Inside' and the album.'

That debut single, 'The Young Own the Town', is the perfect encapsulation of Britpop. It's got the punk energy of the New Wave of New Wave bands like These Animal Men and S*M*A*S*H, the post-punk, angular, art school swagger of Elastica and the 'England my England' shine of 'Modern Life is Rubbish' era Blur. It's the sound of young England in 1995. It should have been a massive hit. 'Inside' was even better with its sweeping guitars, soaring chorus, energy and youthful arrogance, which gave it everything a pop song should have.

CL 'Clive and Alan were fine with us, amiable, we did a lot of pre-production with Clive ripping the songs apart, it was quite a lengthy process. They brought in Elvis Costello's keyboard player, Steve Nieve, to work with us and David Arnold to do strings! It could have been done a lot quicker and on a much smaller budget but instead it took three months and cost a reputed £250,000! Nothing to do with us, it's what Mercury wanted. We were sat in the Studio one day when all these people started to walk in with cellos and violins - a full orchestra, we thought they had got the wrong studio!'

In 1996, the band were invited to perform on one of the biggest shows in the country at the time: The Big Breakfast on Channel 4. It's difficult to imagine now but in the mid-nineties that show was required viewing for anyone with even a passing interest in popular culture. I saw nearly every significant player on the Britpop scene performing and being interviewed on there. Frequently those interviews were conducted by puppets Zig and Zag, which is a fate that befell Soda.

CL *'The Big Breakfast was just one of those things that appeared on our schedule. Not that we weren't excited to be doing it, but it nearly didn't happen as Mercury Records hadn't given it the all clear. I seem to remember Northern Uproar coming out of the cottages just as we were going in! We walked in and there was Zig And Zag! Our first single had gone to No eight in the indie chart and single of the week in the Melody Maker with the video appearing on ITV's The Chart Show and now we were on this big show, it was a really great start for us.*

The troubling thing for us was that radio just didn't want to play the songs, full stop.

We never had one single solitary play of one of our songs on the radio back then. Despite this, people still bought the singles, and even with just that solitary (Big Breakfast) TV appearance to promote the second single, 'Inside' and a UK tour in January 1996 with the Sheds, it went straight into the UK top 100 chart at no 91, and sold 5000 copies in Japan.

We were starting to get the feeling someone somewhere wasn't doing their jobs (not because we weren't selling records) - it just seemed like people were making it up as we went along. We were getting a lot of interest from Japan at that time, it would have made sense to organise a tour to boost our profile but instead management and the label sent us on another UK tour sponsored by Tennants with a band called Baby Chaos. The whole thing was just chaotic, gigs were getting cancelled. Maybe the label were trying to kill us off?'

Lots of bands are uncomfortable with aligning themselves with the Britpop label, because they see it, not unreasonably, as restrictive. It isn't hard to understand why a band like Suede would want to put a bit of distance between themselves and Oasis, for example. But Britpop was an opportunity for lots of bands who wouldn't otherwise have got close to an A&R man to find themselves within touching distance of a spot on Top of the Pops too.

CL 'We were more than happy to have been part of that great 90s musical revolution called 'Britpop' and we still are. Wouldn't change it for the world, despite how things ended for us, it was a wonderful time to be in a band. There hadn't been anything like it in our lives and there will never be anything like it ever again.'

Certain bands suffered a fate worse than death at the hands of certain journalists during Britpop. If Journalist X was sent to see you live and they were not Britpop friendly then it could kill you. Soda were victims of exactly that - they didn't come from London, they didn't have a permanent residence in the Good Mixer and they probably didn't kiss enough arse.

CL 'We felt it most from the NME, they absolutely hated us right from the very start, and for no real reason. They shot us down, slating the singles, giving us bad gig reviews and slagging us off for having a record deal! It's not that we wanted to be liked, we just wanted a fair crack. Something that we had worked very hard for, our dream to get the band and our music to where it deserved to be, which was a lifelong ambition - and certain journalists had the power to destroy that. They even felt it necessary to make personal insults into the way we looked. It's funny really, coming

140

from 'Music Journalists' who made a living off the backs of musicians like us - and who were more than happy to take money from our record company to advertise our singles. They didn't even review the songs. Just slagged us off.'

At that point though the slings and arrows of a few outrageous journalists at the NME could be cast aside because Soda knew that the work they had been doing in the studio was about to deliver something - something that nobody would be able to ignore, not the radio, not the press and not the wider public. They had made a great Britpop album, full to the brim with melodies, hooks, riffs, giddy pop thrills and so much joy it would need to be accompanied by a warning sticker: '*Caution: May Cause Dangerous Levels of Elation*'. Once it was released, the world would listen.

However, what should have been the start of something turned out to be merely the beginning of the end of something. It was April 1996 and Mercury was about to deliver a hammer blow to one of the Britpop scene's brightest hopes.

CL '*When the Album was finished and delivered to the label around April time 1996, we were told that it was going to be shelved. There really was no explanation as to why. I Think Mercury wanted to see how a third single would sell later on in the year. The first two singles had sold pretty well, despite no real big push and no radio play. Looking back on all this twenty years later there were things going on at the label and I think they had lost the plot - they really didn't know what to do with us. I don't think we even had an A&R man at that stage - it also felt like they had put a time limit on us and that time had run out. After the ill-fated Baby Chaos tour we were told we were going back on the road again, this time with Mansun on a full UK tour in the summer of 1996.*

We were pretty enthusiastic in the beginning but cracks had started to show - again it was patchy at best and again gigs were getting cancelled. It turned out we didn't do the majority of the dates we were supposed to do which wasn't anything to do with us.

Mansun were a great band though and we probably felt closer to them than any of the other bands we played with. We did a couple of extra dates in London after the Mansun tour and then played the Guardian stage at the Phoenix festival on the 20th July. Eventually the label released our third, final, and most commercial single to date, 'Dragging You Into my Dreams' in August. They didn't do anything with it, no support at all and that was it, the beginning of the end.'

From the highs of just twelve months earlier when it seemed like they had the world at their feet, Soda had been left reeling and fearing for their future. After a huge financial investment from their label, months of touring, hours in the studio and more effort and energy expended than someone like me could imagine, it was finished. The band headed home, shed a member and decided to try again under a different name.

Early on in this tale, guitarist Liam had suffered a terrifying accident when he was electrocuted on stage during a soundcheck. The incident nearly killed him and left the rest of the band in shock. That incident foreshadowed what was to happen next in this tale. After attracting some interest in their new incarnation from Fire, who were ready to put them into the studio, the unthinkable happened when Liam was diagnosed with leukaemia.

CL 'We had big gigs booked in London, sold out dates, angry concert promoters, but none of that mattered. This was beyond anything that we had experienced before, beyond misfortune, we were facing up to the very real prospect of losing a friend. It was the end for us and the original members of Soda. That was it.'

People moved on.

New lives.

New families.

New goals.

The ties that bound them together had been all but severed.

Then in 2014 there was more tragedy, when lead guitarist Mike Milner suddenly passed away. As proof of how far apart the band had drifted, the sad news only reached the other members by chance. There is something so awful about that. Those bright young things who had been ready to take on the world in 1994 had now been separated to the extent that they could only discover news like this by chance.

CL 'We had had some very brief discussions about releasing the album a few years earlier, however we felt like now would be an ideal opportunity to do so, a tribute to Mike and something for his family. Maybe we could now put a full stop on the Soda story.'

The decision by Mercury not to release 'Artificial Flavours' meant that one of the best bands of the era were relegated to little more than an afterthought. Many 'authorities' on the era wouldn't even be able to tell you the name of any of the singles they released let alone tell you the story of the band.

I spent a lot of my adolescence living in a nowhere town, doing nowhere things. Wandering up and down the High Street, playing pool, kicking a ball about in the lock-ups behind my home and, more than anything, wondering what it would be like to be in a band.

I spent hours and hours in front of the mirror, ignoring the acne, focusing on mimicking the moves of all the boys in all the bands I loved. That meant I would try to do that dance Rick Astley does, whirl and twirl like Andy Bell from Erasure, flail like a demented

Morrissey and pogo like Weller, all while imagining crowds of adoring fans reaching out to me.

Why?

Because I didn't want to have an ordinary life.

I wanted to be *someone*.

It's good being a teenager right?

No, not really - not for the likes of me.

A fish out of water.

Being in a band seemed like it could be both a form of healing and also a satisfying revenge on the small town and small minds that made some days intolerable.

Truthfully though, I knew that it wasn't going to happen - or at least I didn't believe that it could happen for *me*.

So I didn't try.

Listening to Soda is hearing the sound of kids who *did* try, kids who were not prepared to just accept the way things were. There is a ferocity to almost everything - a desperate desire to at least give it a go, knowing that if it didn't work out they could hold their heads up high and say, 'At least we tried'. If things had worked out differently then they would have achieved much more than that.

I tell you what I hear when I listen to 'Artificial Flavour' - it's *hope*. This book is being written during a global pandemic and here in the UK in 2021, we are closing in on a year of lockdown restrictions with a death toll that is terrifying. Hope is in short supply. People can sniff at the idea of finding it in a pop band that nobody has heard of if they like but it is often in the unlikeliest of places that the most important things are found.

Chapter 14

Out of the Shade

Flamingoes

Hitchin.

It's a small town - a nowhere town?

Fewer than forty thousand people live there.

It's probably best known for Valerie Singleton?

Oh, Charles Dickens' daughter and granddaughter came from Hitchin too. But that was a long time ago. And they probably only lived there - they were never real Hitchin folk.

Growing up nowhere gives kids who feel they should be *somewhere* and somebody, a focus that their peers in bigger, brighter and, maybe, better places can't match or even properly understand. I get it, I grew up in a soulless, joyless, empty town that was famous for the smell of linoleum[1] the flooring, not the band.

James and Jude Cook decided fairly early on that life in the confines of Hitchin wasn't really working for them. They wanted out. I suspect it's probably more accurate to say that they yearned for something more than the life they saw people around them living. Maybe, and I can't be sure about this, they felt they deserved something better than what was on offer - plastic pubs, dead end jobs, rowing and fighting, clothes from Next.

---

1. Kirkcaldy in Fife, a seaside town on the East coast of Scotland. Birthplace of Adam Smith and home to Nairns linoleum factory.

So they did what all sensible people do, they started a band.

My first band was called 'The Persuaders', which was, I think we can all agree, a dreadful name for a band, only bettered in the rotten name stakes by the Arctic Monkeys (I'm not arguing about this - it's a shit name for a band) and I deserve to be publically ridiculed about it. James and Jude initially decided that 'The Shade' was a good name for a band, but fortunately they saw the error of their ways in time and plumped for something much better.

That first attempt at becoming musicians featured a brief stint on the drums from Simon Gilbert who would go on to be part of a band who changed British music in many ways and, arguably, created the environment for Britpop to arrive - Suede. As with many teenagers up and down the UK, the arrival of the flamboyant, sexually ambiguous, dangerous and melodious Suede had a seismic impact on James and Jude and they knew that their time had come.

Replacing Simon Gilbert with Kevin Matthews, the brothers set about the process of making their own mark on the world by writing the songs that would eventually emerge as 'Plastic Jewels' in 1995. By that point, what had started with two defiantly English records from Suede and Blur ('Suede' and 'Modern Life is Rubbish') had evolved into a full blown cultural and pop phenomenon. Everywhere you looked there were gangs of bright young things who were hip to the Britpop beat.

My first exposure to The Flamingoes came with the 1994 single 'Disappointed'. The sleeve for that record was worth the purchase price alone as it featured two suburban girls, dressed up, a full can of Ellnet hairspray each and a look of disappointment on their faces as if they both know that whatever terrible nite-klub they are holed up in is beneath them. It positively reeked of fading English glamour and the awfulness of the 1980s. The song itself was everything one could have hoped for - a proper song with a melody, a catchy chorus and sharp guitars and suggested that here we had a band who could make the transition from the fringes to the mainstream.

Listening to that song now and the other singles released in 1994: 'Teenage Emergency' and 'The Chosen Few', it's clear to see that James and Jude (who shared vocal and songwriting duties) were just like me and you. They may have arrived at a point where their sound was going to see them thrown into the 'scene' but they were also a mess, a mass of influences. The obvious things like The Kinks, The Jam and the rawer moments of The Who were there, but there were other things lurking in the shadows, including (gasp!) Nirvana.

'Teenage Emergency' doesn't even try to hide the impact that 'Smells Like Teen Spirit' had clearly had on them. It's in the raw riffs and, if you look hard enough through half-closed eyes, on the sleeve which features a Cobain-lite look-a-like? No? Just me? Fine.

The album 'Plastic Jewels' arrived in 1995 and highlighted the fact that Flamingoes were about so much more than power pop and pop power. Lyrically they were capable of dealing with the types of issues that the likes of Strangelove and Marion were tackling over on the darker side of Britpop, particularly on 'Absent Fathers, Violent Sons' an honest and deeply personal song written by Jude about the impact of divorce, a step-parent and an absent father. Musically the album is a rush - it's brash, melodious, adrenaline fuelled pop music that manages to owe a debt to its influences while never stepping over the line into cover versions.

The problem for so many bands at this point was that while the 'scene' generated label interest and the opportunity to grab a few paragraphs in the NME or Melody Maker, it was also crowded, which made making the leap from the edges to the centre very difficult, particularly after 1994 when the press had already decided who the 'important' bands were. Suede, Pulp, Oasis and Blur dominated the press and radio to such an extent that bands like Flamingoes were starved of the publicity that would have given them a shot at the big time.

It took twelve years for a follow up to 'Plastic Jewels' and it arrived in the form of 'Street Noise Invades the House' which was, as has to be expected after so long, a more mature collection of songs, although I'm not sure what that means to be honest. I guess it means that the rawer, rougher edges of 'Plastic Jewels' had been replaced and refined with something more polished. It's further proof of the enormous talent of both James and Jude, but unfortunately it arrived at the wrong moment - as so many other bands were discovering, the backlash against Britpop meant that the songs, no matter how great, were never going to find favour with certain journalists while the labels had moved on to whatever they thought the next big thing was going to be.

Thankfully both Cook brothers have found other outlets for their creativity in the form of writing fiction, reviews and, in James' case, a soon to be released memoir called 'Memory Songs: a personal journey into the music that shaped the nineties'. The chances of seeing them back on stage again and making new music seem slim right now but maybe with enough love and enough pestering we could see one last hurrah for one of the best bands of the Britpop era; a chance to give them a proper goodbye would be a wonderful thing.

'A 'hate' song about the terrible nights out, which we were too poor to have at the time...'

Emotional rescue.

Pop music at its very finest rescues the damaged from the dreary and drags them to something approaching delirium. It can do that with a riff that rattles bones, a melody that makes you melt and a lyric that leaves you feeling something other than let down. Sometimes, but only sometimes, a pop song comes along that manages to capture all three of these things, and when such a song arrives in your life you will forever hold it close. To let it go would be an act of self-inflicted emotional abuse.

In 1994, I was twenty one years old.

The world was my oyster, I was a grain of sand ready to become a pearl through the gentle agitation of the waves of experience. The disappointment of my teenage years was behind me. I had left behind the nowhere town where I had lived in for the majority of my life, left my parents' home, left the familiar faces and playground bully chases and set out on a new life.

OK, I had chosen to start that new life in Paisley which in 1994 was in the grip of a Benzodiazepine crisis with shell suit clad geezers dropping to the ground like wounded birds all along the main street. It was like a Romero movie. But despite the feeling that I had jumped out of the frying pan and into a Hellish fire I was determined to be free, be free to be what I wanted to be, to have a good time - or at least a better time than I had been having.

Sadly the University of Paisley at this point was not a hotbed of intellectual debate, revolutionary politics, eccentric behaviours or opportunities to explore one's creative desires. Instead it seemed to be almost entirely populated by people who thought beige was the most exciting colour in the world and who wanted nothing more from the experience than to settle down with a boy called Brian, or a girl called Chevonne, before the end of the first term. It was like 'Love Island' but with less steroids and, incredibly, even less hope.

Thankfully this coincided with the blossoming of Britpop from a murmur on the edge of the mainstream cultural conversation to a full blown revolution. Within a matter of weeks my position as an outsider had been flipped and turned upside down and I was, through no real effort of my own, someone who could just about be described as 'cool' - but only just.

At the same time as this, James and Jude Cook were busy trying to write the song, you know *the* song. The song that would lift them from the gutter and place them in the stars. Jude was in his flat in Camden when James arrived with a new song he had been working on. James was obsessed with tempo at this point and the idea of how to write an indie hit that people might actually dance to occupied his thoughts night and day. Their first single, 'Teenage Emergency', had been all pushes, stops and starts.

JUDE COOK *'I was listening to groups like Elastica and The Breeders, songs with a solid 4/4 undercarriage - hearing Simon Price blast out 'Connection' at ULU at nosebleed volume was a real turning point. Basically, we needed a hit. 'Disappointed' was my attempt to write one. It was my attempt to write a song that would get a play at Popscene or Blow Up.'*

The song is a wonderful fusion of influences from the past and the present. From The Beatles to Pavement. All coming together to create a song that was entirely suited to the times.

JAMES COOK *'The curvilinear shape of the verse melody I pinched off The Beatles' 'Get Back' - a rise to form a set up, then a pay off on the fall, but over a descending chord sequence so no-one would know! After days of whittling it like a stick, the chorus, in a different key, emerged. Well, it was a related key, the IV that then, somehow snaked its way back to the home key which is B, the vertiginous key. Both 'Happy' and 'Jumpin' Jack Flash' by the Stones are in B!'*

What dragged the song deep into my heart wasn't the musical magpie charms or the careful construction, at least not at first - no, for me it was the lyrics. Was this the only time in pop music that 'intellectuals' has ever been rhymed with 'perfect pectorals'? Or 'kick in the heart' with 'Exchange and Mart'? Surely it was. It was all very English which, of course, enables it to take its place at the heart of the era.

JAMES COOK *'The words used English or British idioms, such as 'what a waste of time' and 'I don't mind' but I always refused to sing in a mockney accent. The 'Exchange and Mart' line was an attempt at a bit of Lennon-esque nonsense, I always wanted to write in a less pointed, literal way'.*

Despite the Britishness of the lyrics the song is also influenced by one of the best American bands of the era, Pavement. Their quirky but never wacky sensibility and incredible use of language and melody set them apart from the grunge crew and that allowed them to find favour with indie kids like me who were, largely, rejecting anything that came from anywhere outside of Camden at this point.

JAMES COOK *'Then I heard Pavement's 'Cut Your Hair' on Lamacq one night. I knew that I wanted a strong hook at the start of the song so I sort of borrowed it, changed it slightly! But when I brought it to Jude it still wasn't fully formed. It really was a co-write, these were quite rare with us but when they happened they made all the difference.'*

I hadn't heard it before I bought it, I hadn't heard it on the Evening Session or asked the assistant in the store to play it for me. I couldn't have known then that what I was buying was the best single of the Britpop era. How could I?

The best single of the Britpop era.

That's right.

The best.

I know that you love 'Popscene' and 'The Drowners' and 'Babies' and 'Live Forever' and some of you even love 'Wonderwall' and 'Common People' and 'Wake Up Boo' and 'Parklife' and what about The Bluetones and Sleeper and Echobelly and Elastica and Salad and Thurman and The Supernaturals...

I hear you.

I love lots of those songs too.

I adore those bands.

I bought them.

But someone, somewhere, sometime and somehow has to decide which single is the best of the era and I don't see why that someone shouldn't be me here, now and like this.

Everything about 'Disappointed' is perfect.

It perfectly captures the spirit of the era while still managing to be a timeless pop song, a classic piece of English pop music that transcends narrow confines like nationality and language. It is universal.

It should have been the record that broke Flamingoes.

It didn't.

That's not because of the song.

The truth is that the field was overcrowded.

There were new bands, best new bands, best bands in the world, best bands ever in the world ever, cropping up on the front cover of NME, Melody Maker, Select, Vox and goodness where else on an almost weekly basis. This, combined with the mainstream press' fixation on 'the big four' meant that a band like Flamingoes were always going to struggle to get a foothold.

The band agreed that this could have been a hit.

JAMES COOK '*When we took it to Kevin, our drummer, in the rehearsal room there was real excitement. 'Hey, we might have a hit on our hands'. It immediately went to the start of side one on the album running order. Like 'For Tomorrow' it was also the last song written for the album. Then, when we were mixing the album at Wessex, Steve Lamacq played it on the Evening Session back to back with 'Caught by the Fuzz' by Supergrass. We sounded weedy in comparison. Everyone in the room was chuckling at the 'Here comes my mum/she knows what I've done' line, which, I admit, is priceless, but I was a bit jealous, deflated. Disappointed?'*

'Caught by the Fuzz' is a great record and that line is a great line but James is, I think, wrong to feel that 'Disappointed' sounded 'weedy' in comparison. It is a more intricate, delicate, complicated and beautiful record than 'Fuzz' - it's not a 'banger' but it has the ability to put a smile on your face, make your body sway and have you singing along in ways that only the very best songs can.

The very *best* songs.

When the song talks about how hard it is to be aspirational when you don't have a pot to piss in with the line 'It's hard having higher thoughts/when you're on income support' there isn't a kid on a council estate or a working class home anywhere in the world who doesn't get it. Every one of those kids would feel a surge of electricity down their spines when they hear someone saying it on the radio or through their music provider of choice.

Those are the kids like the girls on the front cover of 'Disappointed'. Living lives of quiet desperation, given hope only by the promise of a Friday night out. Never daring to dream that it could be them on Top of the Pops and finding it impossible to believe that there is anything more to life than watching 'pretty people throw up' in the taxi line. Hating the fact that the sort of night out that they really want seems out of reach.

'Disappointed' isn't on the latest greatest hits of Britpop compilation simply because it wasn't actually a hit and it rarely features in lists of the best songs of the era because a lot of people don't even know that it exists.

I know what you are thinking.

'How,' you are thinking, 'can you take a song that so few people bought, that none of the nostalgia pieces even mention, that isn't an anthem, that hasn't been covered by some alt-folk singer from Sandy, Utah and make it your BEST single of the era?'

Let me answer that, if I haven't already, as simply as I can.

I like the people on the fringes, the people who can see the finger of fame beckoning but don't quite reach it, but who then stop and start again. James and Jude Cook started a band, got a deal, played gigs, released an album (a really bloody good album) and then when the spotlight shifted they moved on and became writers, renaissance men.

The song itself is catchy, clever and carefully constructed and creates a concise, clear carbon copy of my own frustrations, hopes and dashed dreams at that moment in time. You could probably say the same thing. There were bigger bands and there were records that defined the era and that sold in the tens of thousands but this is the one that captures my experience of Britpop better than any other.

No more discussion.

'Disappointed', the best single of the Britpop era by one of the best bands of the era.

We're done.

Chapter 15

David Devant

Pop Art and Art as Pop in the delirious world of Mikey B. Georgeson

It is June 1997.

Six weeks earlier, Anthony Charles Lynton Blair, leader of the (New) Labour Party, had taken up residence at 10 Downing Street as Prime Minister.

Soon after that, Noel Gallagher would arrive for a drinks reception in a chocolate brown Rolls-Royce.

The thrill was gone.

The Britpop dream was dying.

The cool had been replaced by something else.

There were still some highs to come but they were really just the last gasps of a scene that had already lasted longer than any of us could ever have imagined.

Things were becoming darker.

There was still hope though.

Back in 1995 I had stumbled across a single by a chap called David Devant.

The single was 'Cookie'.

It sounded a bit like Sparks.

And early Bowie.

And T-Rex.

I really liked it.

The problem was that there was a lot going on in 1995 and it just wasn't possible to keep in touch with every band that drifted into your field of vision or to make any sort of long term commitment to a band. I didn't have A band, I was banding around. Don't judge me. I was young. Nobody had ever explained the concept of safe listening to me. If they had then maybe I would have settled down with David Devant and lived happily ever after.

Who knows.

It would be March 1997 before I reacquainted myself with David.

It turned out that I had got things wrong.

There was no David.

Well, there *was* but he was now dead.

He was a dead magician.

The band were in fact the energy, the soul, the ghost of David pursuing a career in popular music via 'The Vessel'.

His dead wife was involved in this caper as well.

Confused?

You shouldn't be.

'The Vessel' was Mikey Georgeson, an impish genius of melodies.

'Ginger' was a funny song but, crucially, it was not actually a comedy song.

Is there anything worse than a comedy song?

Of course not.

I remember going to see Stewart Lee once and on the stage there was a guitar. Lee is an incredibly gifted comedian and writer and he is genuinely intelligent too. He is one of my favourite performers. I've seen him live several times and always loved it, but not that night. It was the guitar. I knew there was going to be a song and that, rather than do something earnest, he was going to sing a 'funny' song. I didn't like that idea one little bit. I couldn't relax. Eventually the show reached its climax which was, of course, a funny song - he can play guitar, he has a pleasant voice, he has an incredible musical knowledge and a sincere passion for it but this wasn't a touching homage to his heroes or a sincere musical performance: it was a comedy song and it was rubbish.

'Ginger' is a funny and very clever song but it is not a joke.

It has a warm heart.

It is about being different.

It is about being an outsider.

It is about bullying and bullies and the bullied.

I connected instantly.

I did have plans in my head. I had always had plans in my head. I was going to be a writer. I was going to be a singer. I was going to be *someone*. The problem was all of the people who stood in the way of these silly dreams saying things like, 'These are silly dreams'.

I wished they would all just drop dead.

It must have been reviewed in the Melody Maker or NME because although I don't remember seeing a video for it on The Chart Show, I do remember seeing 'The Vessel' for the first time with his Elvis hair, obscenely tight trousers and pencil moustache. He looked so incredible, weird, *other*. I fell hook, line and sinker.

Strangely I didn't connect this with 'Cookie', which had gone missing - maybe I gave it to my girlfriend or some girl I wanted to be my girlfriend. Using its weirdness and obscurity to make me seem cool, hip to the beat and weird in an attempt to woo. It didn't work. Nothing ever worked.

A few weeks later, at the start of June, a second single arrived called 'This Is For Real'.

This was, astonishingly, weirder and better than 'Ginger'.

It had bagpipes.

It was all about Alan's mum and dad and Josephine and Shirley, who had murdered their lovers - a little situation that didn't work out well for their dad.

I don't think there is any metaphor being employed or deployed here.

I think it is just a strange, silly, slightly wonky little pop song, like 'The Laughing Gnome' but good.

What was becoming increasingly obvious was that David Devant and His Spirit Wife were making me think a little more than most bands. There was the whole concept behind the name, which was a nod, an ode, a hymn to vaudeville and a loving look back at a time that was very different to the one they existed in. It was backwards looking but not in an attempt to recreate or mimic what had gone before, instead, it seemed, it was a prop, a tool, a vehicle that they could use for something slightly grander than being another Britpop band. Or any sort of band.

I had a feeling that maybe this was something more than pop music.

I don't know if I can say it.

People come over all peculiar when you say it.

I *have* to say it though.

This was pop as art.

Pop-art.

Art-pop.

Pop made by an artist.

Or art made by a popist.

It was, I think, high-brow masquerading as low-brow.

Or maybe it was low-brow masquerading as high-brow.

Or maybe it was just all a bit of a lark?

A situationist prank wrapped up in a situation comedy about a pop band?

I may be overthinking.

Or not thinking enough.

> *'He is a dead conjurer. She is representative of your spirit wife, my spirit wife. She is the inner muse who sends us a tingle down our spine. We want to become icons and, musically, we are just about the history of pop music.'*
>
> (The Vessel, Channel 5, 1997)

That is how Mikey Georgeson attempted to explain David Devant and His Spirit Wife to Jonathan Coleman.

Dead conjurers.

Spirit wives.

Muses.

History.

To Jonathan Coleman.

It takes a certain type of confidence, or madness, to use a magazine feature on national television to sell your art-pop/pop-art vision like that.

At around the same time I also saw The Vessel grate a carrot on 'Alternative Nation'.

Yes I did.

It wasn't just the band's story that contained magic, the music was laced through with the sort of divination and wizardry that only comes from those rare moments of pop alchemy when base materials like a drum kit, a bass guitar and a lead guitar are infused with some other element and BIFF BANG POW, you've got pure pop gold.

Debut album 'Work, Lovelife, Miscellaneous' arrived in the middle of June and it was everything one could have hoped for. Twelve songs made from storytelling, melody, melancholy, joy, nonsense and hope. Twelve songs that, after only one listen, you would never be able to forget. Each one a little nugget of pop gold. Each one capable of making you smile, laugh and dance and then lift the needle so that you could do it all again.

Each song has a line, a word, a turn of phrase that sticks and unsticks you. There are songs about death and romance and fame and relationships and family and loneliness and connecting and so much more. There are songs of love and wonder. All crafted with the care and attention to detail of an artist.

There is that word again.

It shouldn't really be a surprise of course, Georgeson *is* an artist. A real one. A painter and an illustrator using various mediums to present various ideas. He may even be, whisper it, a bona fide eccentric.

This is a compliment of course.

Like Edith Sitwell but operating in pop and not modernist poetry.

Much as I love so many of the Britpop bands, and so many pop bands in general, it is difficult to imagine any of them saying something like this:

> '*I believe in magic and the power of following passions to lead to instances of backwards causality. In his autobiography there is an illustration of Devant making a ghost disappear 'in front of a critical audience' which, as a title alone, has parallels to painting pictures if you ask me. About the time Harry Pye first suggested time was right for a Devant themed show, I was sorting through some books I hadn't touched since they had come into my possession via my polymath cousin, Ricky Rhubarb. The first chapter of the first book was a sketch of Augustus John basically saying he was a bit hit or miss but when his work clicked 'one stares at it with amazement as if this were a Maskelyne and Devant trick and one saw a box floating in mid air'. My jaw slackened and I read on to discover the next chapter was a poetical tiptoe through the dichotomy of magic and science. Reaching for my lighter I found it gone. Coincidence? No, I don't smoke any more.*'
>
> ('My Magic Life', Exhibition Catalogue, 2008)

Read it again.

It's perfect.

A carefully constructed joke and then a pull back and reveal.

But there was more too - there was also inspiration, art and magic.

That was what set David Devant and his Spirit Wife apart, the fact that while there was very definitely light on the surface, there was also a parallel universe in their work. There was an attempt to reinvent the wheel of pop with the careful use and manipulation of the norms of the genre, creating something fresh from something that was in danger of becoming stale. A shove towards anomie, the breaking down of the societal norms of popular culture before replacing them with something new, different and magical. Listening to 'Work, Lovelife, Miscellaneous' now, twenty-two years later, is like stepping into a ballroom from a different era - things sound familiar and yet remain indescribable, untouchable.

Incredibly, though, this is only a tiny part of the tale.

There were other songs before 'Work, Lovelife, Miscellaneous' and there would be others afterwards too.

Then there were the live shows - and *what* shows they were.

And Mr Solo.

And Mikey Georgeson and the Civilised Scene.

Oh and Glam Chops and Carfax too.

We will get to all of that at some point I'm sure.

It's time this tale was told.

With kindness.

Chapter 16

We'll Get What We Deserve

Despite lazy comparisons to The Smiths, Gene were resolutely, defiantly, their own thing. They were sharp dressers and smart musicians.

This isn't a story of boy meets girl.

No.

Wait.

A long time ago…

No, that's no good either. Too clichéd.

Let me think about this.

O.K, this time.

He was looking for something, looking for someone.

No. Too impersonal. This has to be personal. This *is* personal.

One more try.

I was looking for something, looking for someone and then I found *them*, but really I found *him*.

Perfect.

Before we really get into this, I think we should start in the middle.

I had managed to blag my way backstage at The Venue in Edinburgh when Gene played there while on their 'Revelations' tour. It was a small venue but they were a big band. They had been on the telly and everything. I would become a bit obsessed with them. I fell, utterly, for the 'new Smiths' label that had been hung (not entirely unfairly) around their respective necks since the release of their debut single. Thanks to bad timing on the part of my parents, I had not been born in time to be old enough to be aware of The Smiths when they were still a band. I had come to them after they had split and hadn't ever really got over that fact. I transferred all of my upset over that into an obsession with Gene - they would be my Smiths.

I am backstage then. Everyone is being very friendly to me and I eventually strike up a conversation with Martin Rossiter. He is incredibly charming. Nice. Funny. Call me silly but I think we sort of hit it off in that way that so rarely happens. I got the distinct impression that we could be friends. Of course, everybody who ever meets one of his or her idols feels that way but...

The next day I meet up with Martin as the band are staying in Edinburgh for one more night before heading off to the next gig on the tour. We go out for a bite to eat. Pizza Express, if you are interested. It's a nice evening. We have things in common. This is beginning to sound like the early stages of a romance. I suppose that it was in a way. I certainly loved Gene and, by extension, I loved Martin. Before the band leave town, he invites me to attend their gig at the Leadmill in Sheffield. It's a fair old journey but I don't have anything better to do so I agree.

After that gig, I am introduced to a fabulous character by the name of Trotsky. He is, like me, a music obsessive and a skinhead. We have been mates ever since. Martin has known Trotsky since they worked in an Our Price together some years ago. I like the fact that he's stayed in touch with someone from a time before the fickle finger of fame pointed at him, it suggests a certain integrity. After that, I met up with Martin and his wife (a more beautiful person on the outside and the inside you would struggle to meet) a few times - we even went ten-pin bowling on one occasion. I won.

Then we rather drifted apart a bit. We were never friends of course; at best, I was an acquaintance, a fleeting character in the background of the soap opera of a Britpop star's life during the

1990s. I would wager that Martin has no memory of any of this having taken place. Who could blame him for that? Not me. I am not particularly memorable. Most of you will already have forgotten me by the time you get to the end of this sentence - see.

The debut single from Gene arrived in 1994. It was 'For the Dead' and it was the first single of the Britpop era that obviously owed a debt to The Smiths. I know that the budget Smiths thing is a bit of a dial-a-cliché where Gene are concerned but with this single, it was accurate. I have a very clear memory of watching the video for 'For the Dead' on the ITV Chart Show one Saturday morning. It is a genuinely dark and sad song, entirely at odds with the 'cor blimey, geezer' offerings of many of the Britpop bands. There was very little sun-shee-ine in the lyrics of 'For the Dead', instead it traded in filth, isolation, cold and darkness and was, very clearly, a world away from girls who liked boys who liked girls who liked etc.

> *'Intelligence isn't to be ignored. Articulacy isn't to be ignored.'*
>
> (Martin Rossiter)

> *'Our lyrics have a lot of depth to them. Most bands don't pay enough attention to lyric writing and Martin does it with a lot of gusto and damn sight more sophistication than anybody I know of.'*
>
> (Steve Mason)

That intelligence, articulacy, sophistication and gusto was echoed in the music that Steve Mason (guitar and, never forget, haircut), Kevin Miles (bass) and Matt 'the hat' James (drums) crafted around the words. As a result, Gene quickly became one of the best known live acts on the nascent Britpop scene, so much so that NME journalists Keith Cameron and Roy Wilkinson set up a record label, Costermonger, with the sole purpose of promoting them to a wider audience. They would release 'For the Dead' as a double a-side with 'Child's Body' (a song that caused some controversy thanks to the line 'Give me, your child's body' ignoring the fact that the song was about the horrors of anorexia, certain tabloid types attempted to paint it as being about something a lot more sinister) and release it as an ultra-limited 7" single. The run of 1,994 copies sold out within two days and copies were quickly selling for several times the purchase price - my copy cost me £30.

A second single, 'Be My Light, Be My Guide', was released shortly after this and it too proved a big hit with the indie kids of the Britpop scene. Here was a band, it appeared, who had something to say and were keen to say it with as much verve, guts and guile as they could manage. 'Be My Light' was a twisted hymn to drunken nights out that were fuelled by regret and shame more than lust and desire.

Two more singles ('Haunted by You' and 'Sleep Well Tonight') preceded the debut album 'Olympian', which arrived on the shelves in 1995. I was actually waiting outside the tiny record shop in town before it opened. I wanted to be one of the first people to own a copy. I had a feeling that 'Olympian' was going to be a rallying call to the grotesquely lonely and also the first step on the journey to world domination for a band that I had grown to love in a ridiculously short amount of time.

Back in my room, I hit play and waited.

First up was 'Haunted by You', which I already knew. Every slightly awkward, unusual and acne ridden adolescent boy with no stomach for sport (and certainly with no sporting ability) knows the harm that words can cause. I was once followed around the playground when I was in my fourth year of secondary school by a girl in the first year screaming 'Pizza Pus' (pus is a charming Scottish word for face) at me for the duration of the lunch break until eventually I had to take shelter in the toilets. I know, I know, it is hardly the equivalent of the treatment that Gripper Stebson handed out to Roland Browning in 'Grange Hill' but still, it was embarrassing and confusing. Here we are thirty years later and I still remember it. Anyhoo - your words, they cannot harm me now.

What was already obvious was that the comparisons with The Smiths were simply devious, truculent and unreliable statements from music journalists who hadn't listened to Gene or, in all likelihood, The Smiths either.

From the earliest moments of the Gene tale, Rossiter had been unambiguous about his sexuality and told Jon Wilde in an interview with Sabotage Times in 2012:

> *'I wasn't remotely interested in a game of hide and seek with the media. I'd have considered that to be a betrayal of the people who'd gone before me and fought for gay rights. I couldn't be doing with some long running 'is he or isn't he?' debate because that would have been profoundly boring. I didn't want to be Michael Stipe or Morrissey. Admitting that I was bisexual didn't harm me in the slightest. In the main my sexuality was irrelevant to the songs.'*

My favourite track on 'Olympian' is the sweet and tender, giddy rockabilly of 'Still Can't Find the 'Phone' complete with its nod to the King, Elvis himself, in Martin's 'uh-huh-huh' at the end of the first verse. Many years later I asked him to make me a tape of Elvis songs because, growing up in a Mod household I hadn't really been aware of him. When that tape arrived in the post, it kicked off with 'If I Can Dream' which, almost instantly, became one of my favourite songs. That song was also covered by fellow outsiders, Strangelove, with Patrick Duff dedicating it to his 'mama'. Funny old world innit.

'And since Space is divisible in infinitum, and Matter is not necessarily in all places, it may be also allow'd that God is able to create Particles of Matter of several Sizes and Figures, and in several Proportions to Space, and perhaps of different Densities and Forces, and thereby to vary the Laws of Nature, and make Worlds of several sorts in several Parts of the Universe. At least, I see nothing of Contradiction in all this.'

(Isaac Newton, 'Opticks', 1704)

The theory of multiverse is open to debate and criticism of course but if we can accept, just for the sake of argument, that there may well be other, infinite, universes where all possibilities are being played out, then I would like to suggest that it isn't impossible that somewhere, sometime, somehow there is another, alternate world where 'Olympian' is number one in the charts and it will forever be number one.

'Olympian' is the quintessential Gene song. It begins with a whisper of 'Give me something I can hold, with that something I will grow', and then a piano chimes, a guitar gently weeps and drums roll gently like waves lapping against the shore. It grows more confident, becomes more assured - formidable, not afraid. Finally it becomes an anthem, the sort of song that could only ever be properly at home in front of thousands, tens of thousands, of adoring and adorable apostles. 'I could only be normal with you,' sings Rossiter and we all cry back: 'There is no such thing as normal.' It's a passionate plea from a broken heart that is demanding that we piece it back together.

One of the most striking aspects of the British music scene in the 1990s was the elevation of the humble b-side from its original position of filler to the home of songs that could easily have been hit records in their own right. Suede released a double-album of their b-sides that many people believe is their finest collection of songs. Oasis threw songs that could have been number one records on their b-sides, while Blur used the space to deliver curious artefacts and glimpses of future directions. Gene were no different and the b-sides from the singles leading up to 'Olympian' were fabulous things: 'Child's Body', 'This is Not my Crime', 'I Can't Help Myself', 'Sick, Sober and Sorry', 'Do You Want to Hear it From Me?', 'How Much For Love?', 'I Can't Decide if She Really Loves Me' and 'To See the Lights' were all fine examples of the gifts of Gene, a fact the band and their label clearly recognised as they released them all together on 'To See the Lights' in 1997, an album that made it into the top twenty.

It is a fact, universally acknowledged by this time, that Gene were one of the finest live acts of their day. Whereas some people saw Rossiter as a fey, winsome, twee(dy) character, the truth was that he was a muscular live performer, a man who could win over even the most hostile of crowds and hold them in the palm of his hand. The band were equally powerful live performers, ensuring that the sound and the fury remained constant regardless of whether they were in King Tuts Wah Wah Hut in Glasgow or the Brixton Academy. All of this combined to ensure that the Gene fanbase was large and loyal.

What came next was nothing less than a heartbreaking work of staggering genius.

'Drawn to the Deep End' is the most devastatingly honest and emotionally brutal album of the nineties.

While critics were working themselves into a frenzy over Radiodead and their maudlin mumblings, Gene quietly released a flawless set of songs that spoke directly to the heart while running their immaculate sonic fingers across your brow to soothe you.

Instead of blowing their marketing budget on a cocaine fuelled blow-out at a trendy London nite-klub, Gene took the album to the people at a series of playback evenings in the most intimate of venues. The band were there, each song was introduced and then played with video footage to accompany them. I was there for the Glasgow date at the Old Athenaeum, a former cinema with a fading glamour that seemed to perfectly suit the songs and the album artwork. During the audience Q&A, I asked what Martin's thoughts were about Oscar Wilde's pronouncement that 'Talent borrows, genius steals' to which he replied:

> *'Well, all I can really say is that I do use the library but I always return the books.'*

It's difficult to see this as anything other than firm evidence for the ready wit of Gene's leader and my own inability ever to be anything other than a bit less witty than everyone else in the room.

The album opens with 'New Amusements' and the hiss and crackle of a guitar being hooked up to a speaker then a throbbing, pulsating bass line and a simple piano coda while a guitar part begins to build. Rossiter's background whisper is nearly drowned by the sound before a furious, nearly hysterical rhythm bursts from the disquieting stillness. It's a mixed up, muddled up, shook up tune with a filthy and furious lyric. It also highlights the fact that Gene possessed not just one of the most curious and quotable singers of his generation but an equally gifted set of musicians, with Steve Mason the nearly too Mod for Mod guitarist playing the laddish foil to Rossiter's more fey sensibilities, Matt 'the hat' James on drums and Kevin Miles on bass.

'Is this song about shagging?' is, according to Rossiter himself, the question he was asked by his own mother when she first heard the next track 'Fighting Fit'. He had to confirm that it was indeed about the glories and delicious pains of the beast with two backs - it would have been a futile exercise to try and deny it.

The first time I heard 'Where Are They Now?' all of the comparisons with The Smiths made sense, not because it sounded like them (the truth is that Gene always sounded just like Gene) but because the sense of yearning, the desire to be loved and to be able to love, which was so beautifully and brilliantly captured in the lyrics, was the match of anything that Morrissey had ever committed to vinyl.

Who is 'HoHo McGann'[1]? is the question on the lips of many after 'Speak To Me Someone' reaches its climax. I'm being frivolous of course, because that is how British men deal with the sort of truth and beauty that hits you square in the face when you listen to something like this. I was still at university when 'Drawn to the Deep End' arrived and I was miserable. I was in a long distance relationship that had turned sour and toxic and I was miles away from my friends and my family. I so desperately wanted someone to smash into me, to hold me and to tell me I would dream again.

When Martin encouraged us all to tell the people we prize most that we love them in 'We Could be Kings' I did exactly that. I picked up the landline (or the 'phone as it was known then) and started to dial.

'Chris? It's Max. I just wanted to let you know…well…I just wanted to say…I love you. Night mate.'

'Ben, Max. I want you to know that I love you.'

'Keith, it's me, Max. Yeah, I'm fine. Listen. I love you.'

I called everyone I knew who had ever been friendly towards me, never mind had ever been an actual friend and told them that I loved them. It felt wonderful. Of course I know that love isn't just about 'saying' and that it's actually 'showing' that really matters but it's still important to let people know sometimes.

'Why I Was Born' is another love song, another hymn to friendship, to intimacy, to longing. The idea of not actually being

---

1. A line in the song which includes the words 'home again' is sung by Rossiter in such a way that it sounds like he is, in fact, singing 'Hoho McGann'.

alive until twenty five that Rossiter sings about was of huge comfort to me as I was twenty four and knew that, at best, my life up to that point had been half-lived and could only really be measured out in bus stops and rain. The idea that things might be about to actually *start* filled me with the hope of the hopeless.

It happened a long time ago now.

It seems like it was yesterday.

The decision to self-harm wasn't one that had always been in my mind. I hadn't ever thought about it. I wasn't the type. Whatever the type was - or is. After I had done it I drove myself to triage and was patched up by a very sympathetic nurse before being sent home after an overworked doctor asked me if I felt suicidal. I didn't. I felt *desperate*? I felt a bit disconnected. I felt a bit sad. On the drive home, I wondered what this meant and thought about the bit in 'Long Sleeves for the Summer' when Rossiter sings about how much hurt simply living can bring, which is truer than so many realise.

In an album filled to the point of overflowing with songs about the need to be loved, the need for love, the need to show love and the need to fill the aching void that passes as a heart, the most delicate and sincere is 'Save Me, I'm Yours'. It's the highlight of a magnificent suite of songs. Each note embraces the lonely and each line comforts the ailing and the failing. It's lovely and warm and raw and *everything*.

Something darker this way comes in the shape of the deeply unsettling 'Voice Of The Father'. The horror of childhood nightmares that are actually childhood memories is laid bare as Rossiter sings of bad dreams being made real, closed doors that terrify and time as a sinister force that can devour. It's a very unsettling song made more so by the pounding, brutal, forceful music that drives it. The theme of domestic abuse is carried on in 'The Accidental' where a victim takes matters into their own hands with a flashing blade.

'I Love You, What Are You?' is an invitation to come and find true love in arms that could be the 'home you never had'. It's a welcome moment of hope after the despair of so much of what has preceded it, with Rossiter demanding that you carry on because, well, life will do so anyway. That glimmer of hope is echoed by the tender heart of 'Sub Rosa'. Perversely though, this moment of charm ends with a reprise of the opening sonic assault of 'New Amusements' where the amps are turned up to eleven which, of course, is one more than ten.

> *'I struggled to listen to [Drawn To The Deep End] because of the production. It was a little bit too hi-fi and I didn't like my voice on the record.'*[2]

That, I think, is the difference between the artist and the fan - the constant need to see ways in which things can be improved, a desire to move forwards. For me 'Drawn to the Deep End' is faultless.

If 'Drawn to the Deep End' was an album that spoke directly to the broken and the lonely then 'Revelations' offered a glimpse into the soul of man under capitalism. It is one of the most overtly political albums of the nineties. Just a few years earlier, Noel Gallagher had been quaffing champagne inside 10 Downing Street with Tony Blair and the whole country had bought into the New Labour vision - things could only get better had been the campaign promise after all. For Rossiter, a devout, radical socialist, the whole thing was a sham and he was eager to let everyone involved in the project know exactly what he thought. To accompany this political fury, Rossiter ditched his foppish locks and returned with his head shaved, possibly a nod to 80s political agitators and redder than red socialists The Redskins.

---

2. Martin Rossiter, The Argus, 2013

Epistolary. Apocalyptic. Prophetic.

Gene's book of revelations (I know that in the Bible it is the Book of Revelation) is a letter to the political class, it is filled with visions of the end of socialism and offers a vision of what lies in wait for the Labour Party, all delivered with the sort of pop 'n' roll that we had grown to love. This of course casts Martin as some sort of saintly figure. The Catholic Saint Martin was one who cared for all people regardless of race or wealth - our Martin would approve.

Early on in my wife's pregnancy, we had a bit of a scare and we ended up visiting the hospital in the early hours of the morning to get some help. As we sat waiting for several hours all of the most awful thoughts filled our heads; what will we do if we've lost the baby was chief among them. It was a long and upsetting night. We hardly spoke a word. When we eventually saw someone and were sent home with relatively comforting words we sat in the car and cried.

There was only one song I wanted to hear, only one song that would work. 'Little Child' was that song. It is a song from a father to a child, an attempt to make clear that no matter what might unfold in life, some things are forever, like the love of a parent. I felt instantly soothed.

While the album was solid, it is also true to say that it was unremarkable. It was the first time that I found myself ready to lift the needle after just one listen and move on to the next track. That sounds like a criticism but it is simply a comment on how high the mark had been set by the previous albums, as after all, most albums see you stabbing at the skip button at least once.

> *'Only when we got to Gretna Green did we realise that Polydor had disembarked at Crewe.'*
>
> (Martin Rossiter)

It was clear to the band that Polydor had lost interest in Gene and had, consequently, failed to promote 'Revelations' with as much gusto as it deserved. It is an album that, better than any of their others, captures the power of Gene live. One cannot help but feel that the rushed nature of the recording process (it took just a month to complete) and a lack of any real marketing was simply an attempt by Polydor to ease Gene towards the exit. This isn't an unfamiliar tale for British bands in 1999, when the record labels felt, rightly or wrongly, that the time was up for Britpop and so any band seen to be a part of that moment found themselves cast adrift.

The band carried on as a live entity throughout 2000 and, famously, became one of the first acts to see the potential of the internet when they performed a webcast live from the Troubador in Los Angeles to around 60,000 people worldwide. I wasn't one of them as the internet hadn't quite made it into my life at that stage. That show was also released as the live album 'Rising for Sunset' which featured songs from all three albums and three new songs: 'Does he Have a Name?', 'Rising for Sunset' and 'Somewhere in the World'. It was a snapshot of a band at a crossroads - clearly they still had 'it' and they still had a massive fanbase but could they persuade anyone else to back them?

The answer to that question was *not really*. Instead, Gene took the plunge and self-released what was to be their final album 'Libertine' on their own Sub-Rosa Records label. It reached number 92 in the charts in 2001 and signalled the end for a band who were not just loved but *adored* by their followers.

Chapter 17

The Darkness Inside

Marion - Strangelove

It wasn't all cigarettes and alcohol, cups of tea and the delights of a night out in the Good Mixer during the Britpop years. Bands emerged who traded in darker themes, turbulent times and broken bodies and hearts. For the moments when you needed someone to soothe you through something more tangible than sympathetic looks and mild best wishes, there were Marion and Strangelove.

> *'I've experienced violence,' he shudders. 'And it's made me scared of ever being violent, or ever having a family, or ever having a wife, or ever having a drink.'*[1]
>
> *'Who is the worst person you've ever met?' 'Erm... my dad.'*[2]

When Marion released their debut single 'Violent Men' in 1994 it appeared to tell the tale of a frightened girl, trapped in a home where violence was a terrifying part of her everyday life. It was a slice of the darker side of life that few other bands at that time were dealing with. Looking back at the comments in the Melody Maker, made some three months before the single was released, it is clear that the frightened girl in the song was, in fact, Harding. That ability to write so honestly and yet through

---

1. Jaime Harding, Melody Maker, 12 March 1994
2. Jaime Harding, NME, June 1994

the eyes of another, almost viewing his own life as an out of body experience, set Harding apart from the 'knees up muvver brahn' of some other writers of the time. That is not a criticism of the upbeat, the frivolous or the slight but is merely an observation of what made Marion separate from many of their peers.

From the very early stages of the Marion story comparisons were being made with The Smiths and Joy Division. It's easy to see why. Manchester, a troubled childhood, an intensity in the sound, lyrical themes and, overall, honesty about the side of life that so many of us know but few of us feel confident, or comfortable, discussing. There were also some very direct links to The Smiths, particularly their relationship with Joe Moss. Moss, of course, had managed The Smiths and when he received an early demo from Marion he offered his services to them, even allowing them to rehearse in the basement of The Night and Day Cafe in Manchester's Northern Quarter. The links between the two bands were cemented when Marion were awarded the support slot on Morrissey's UK tour in 1995.

> *'Were we ever big Smiths fans? No, not really. We were too young, man. I mean, Morrissey's done good stuff...but when did The Smiths split? 1987? We were twelve years old. We're not into the past, we're into the future and the present.'* [3]

Marion had existed, in one form or another, since Jaime Harding was eleven. *'I started singing at school, and Keith, my best mate, would have to listen to me saying 'Hey, look at these lyrics – 'the past is our only mistake'! And he'd be going 'Get out of it...what the fuck are you on about?'.*

---

3. Jaime Harding, NME June 1994

It's rare, I think, for anyone so young to know, with such absolute certainty, that they want to be an artist of any description and then to pursue that path. It certainly wasn't an easy path for this gang of outsiders from Macclesfield. Their hometown during the 1980s, like so much of the North, was gritty, which meant that aspiring to any kind of better future would have been a challenge.

After Jaime read 'Morrissey and Marr: The Severed Alliance' he forged a friendship with Joe Moss, having been impressed by the way Moss was portrayed. The band of five comprised Harding on vocals, Anthony Grantham and Phil Cunningham on guitars, Murad Mousa on drums and Julian Phillips on bass. Tucked away in that basement rehearsal space in the Northern Quarter they began to become Marion. After nine months of practicing, tweaking, fine tuning and repeating they were ready for London shows. They were signed by Rough Trade and released 'Violent Men' which sparked a bidding war that was eventually won by London Records. Their time had come.

In January 1995 I attended the Glasgow leg of the NME 'Brat Pack' tour at the Garage on Sauchiehall Street. Marion were the main draw on a bill that also included Veruca Salt, 60ft Dolls and Skunk Anansie. What I witnessed that night was something that borders on the indescribable. They were ferocious. Each song was thrown at the audience with a thunderous, nearly tangible, fireball of rage, mania, love and desire. I couldn't take my eyes off Harding. He danced with the microphone stand, he prowled the stage, he leered, he winked, and he owned the stage, the venue and the night. I fell head over heels in love.

A month later I was in Motherwell to see Morrissey. Marion were the support act. This time they had to contend with an audience who actively did not want to see them. As the crowd chanted the name of Morrissey through the opening numbers of their set I could see Jaime's face darkening. 'In six months, you'll all be paying to see US!' he sneered. Absolute belief. It can't be arrogance when you really are that good. The crowd shut their mouths and by the end of the set you could sense that people were torn - they had come to see the Emperor but had witnessed his heir and they wanted to pay tribute.

'Sleep' was released in February 1995. An NME review at the time declared that Marion were 'eminently ignorable' which is the sort of catty, snarky and sarcastic comment that we had all come to grow to loathe in the music press at that time. The truth was that nobody was ignoring Marion. Their concerts sold out, crowds were falling at their feet, there wasn't a student union or indie club in the land who were not playing their records and anyone who was watching knew that something big was looming on the horizon.

When 'Toys For Boys' was released a few months later it served as further evidence that this was a band who could really be *something*. The music press had decided to deride them though and there were further bitter, mean and spiteful reviews, most noticeably from the NME (again) who seemed to have decided that Marion were 'out'. Ironically, boys and girls up and down the country who really knew what it was like to be 'out' were resolutely, defiantly 'in' when it came to Marion.

Thankfully the editor of the live desk at the NME hadn't received the memo and it was here that the truth of Marion could be found. *'What Marion add to this is a fury of distilled malevolence. When Jaime half croons, half taunts 'Sometimes it feels so nice to laugh at you when you cry' in a cataclysmic 'Late Gate Show', it's almost as if his rage is being taken out on someone, anyone who happens to be caught in the flood of emotions'.*

It would be early 1996 before the debut album 'This World and Body' finally arrived. The question was would it be worth the wait? The answer, of course, was yes. It had been obvious from the singles and live shows that Marion were a band where each member had put the hours in, no blaggers, no part-timers, nobody

178

in just because they looked the part. Listening to the album three things leap out at you: Jaime is a fine singer and songwriter, Phil Cunningham is a fabulous guitarist and the rhythm section were much more than bodies in the studio. The fact that the album reached the top ten in its first week of release proves that there was 'something' about Marion.

The songs are filled with desire, longing, angst, passion, rage, love and death. The guitars swoop and slide. The bass rolls and rumbles. The voice soars, yelps, whispers, sighs and screams. The drums beat, pound and rattle your bones. The singles 'Sleep', 'Let's All Go Together', 'Toys for Boys' and 'Time' were all present and correct, with only 'Violent Men' absent. The truth of the matter is that there were at least another three songs that could have been singles: 'Fallen Through', 'The Only Way' (which did get a release on a Club Spangle EP) and 'I Stopped Dancing' are all songs that would make a 'Best of' compilation for dozens of other better known and more successful acts.

> *'The band is something we all need to do. When I write, I write lyrics that deal with emotions and I channel all my emotions into songs. Without it I would be a sad-arse like I was before Marion gave me the opportunity of doing this full-time for the rest of my life.'*[4]

The promotion for 'This World and Body' included nearly eighteen months of touring. Up and down the UK, the States and Europe. Solo shows. Support slots. Festivals. For people in the crowd, live performance looks like the best job in the world, hundreds of adoring fans, people dancing and singing to the songs you've written, posters on the wall, autographs - it's glamorous.

---

4. Jaime Harding, RAW, 1996

What do you do for the other twenty three hours when you are not on stage or when you don't have a show at all? For many people in bands the answer is, often tragically, drugs. Lots and lots of drugs. Then more drugs.

> *'Then I started doing way too many drugs – the wrong drugs. I'd always used speed and cocaine but the heroin really took hold round the making of 'The Program'. Johnny hated it because he'd dealt with that part of his life a long time ago. We were supposed to get Chrissie Hynde in for backing vocals but she'd had bandmates who'd died from drug use and she'd have been disgusted. Johnny and the band, and Joe, stuck by me for way longer than they should have. But by the time the record was finished, I was good for nothing.'*[5]

'I was good for nothing.'

Oscar Wilde said that 'Nothing should be beyond hope, life is hope' and when one thinks of a young man who before his life has really begun thinking that he is good for nothing, it's enough to make you weep. The cliché of the tortured artist is one that is all too familiar and, I think, is applied far too freely to people who don't really know what it means to suffer. In the case of Jaime, I think he really is a man who has demons, who has experienced pain and who is simply trying to cope, to make sense of it all.

By the time the band started working on the follow up to 'This World and Body' tensions were already all too evident. Joe Moss had persuaded Johnny Marr to come on board as producer. It should have been a brilliant moment - they were making a record that they hoped would shift them from the fringes to the forefront

---

5. Jaime Harding

of the music scene. That things didn't go that way is no reflection on the album as it was another tremendous record.

'The Program' is a huge leap forward from an already fairly impressive starting point. The problem is that the heroin issue was overshadowing the music. Shortly after the release of the lead single from the album, 'Miyako Hideaway', the NME ran a full page interview with Jaime entitled 'Jaime's Addiction'. Three quarters of that interview is devoted to discussing drugs. A live review in the same journal a few weeks later was entitled 'The Drugs Didn't Work'. Next up was an article in the Melody Maker, 'Running with the Smack'. Are you getting the picture?

'Miyako Hideaway' was released in March 1998 and was destined to be the last single from Marion. A year later and Marion were a memory. A band who had promised so much, a band who had meant so much to a loyal gaggle of disciples, a band who had faced down the snide comments of the music press, a band with more verve, vim and vigour than many of their peers, a band who meant it - gone.

Here's a funny thing about drugs, not funny 'ha ha' but funny peculiar. They tend to get in the way of things. Relationships. Careers. Hopes. Dreams. Ambitions. All break apart on the rocks that form the shoreline of the addict's life. Lies, deceit, betrayal, crime, misdemeanours - these are the things that, more often than not, fill the life of the soul who has committed his life, albeit inadvertently, to drugs. Especially heroin.

In the years following the demise of Marion there have been sporadic highs in the form of reunions, live shows, new line-ups and anniversaries. Sadly they would all turn out to be reminders of what once was and what might have been rather than an actual return to form. The details of what has happened in the life of Jaime are there for those who are interested.

I'm not.

The past is the past.

A foreign country.

I'm interested in the future.

One hundred and fifty miles away from Jaime and the boys in Marion lies Bristol. Bristol isn't a city that enjoys the sort of attention for music that the likes of Glasgow, Manchester, Liverpool, Sheffield and London do. That's unfair because over the years there have been several really interesting, peculiar, groundbreaking and influential acts to have crawled from the West Country to stardom. The Brilliant Corners, Portishead, Massive Attack, The Pop Group, Ben Gunstone and Tricky are a few of the Brizzle contingent to have made their way into the ears and hearts of the nation. A variety of sounds and styles all bound together by a willingness to look at the darker side of life. If misery loves company it must feel very much at home in the home of the outrageous and free that is Bristol.

Strangelove were Bristol's contribution to Britpop. Except they were never really Britpop, they were something else. Something *other*. Alongside Marion they presented an alternative vision of what British pop was: eccentric, arty, edgy, troubled and yet still wedded to the notion of motion and emotion in the music.

Melody makers each and every one.

Soundtracks to the lives of others.

'*Get in the car, you're going to be a pop star.*'[6]

After this introduction, David Francolini bundled Patrick Duff into the back of his car and they headed to an attic room rehearsal space where they recorded their first song. Less than a year later Strangelove released the 'Visionary' EP. A collection of four songs that sounded exactly like - well, that was the thing, they didn't sound like anything or anyone else. They were gothic without being goth, they were grand and yet intimate, they were bold but

---

6. This, according to the legend, is how David Francolini introduced himself to a young Patrick Duff while he was busking in Bristol.

delicate. The only thing they sounded like was Strangelove and, at that point, nobody knew who, or what, that was.

They soon would.

I remember hearing 'Time for the Rest of Your Life', the lead single from the debut album of the same name, and feeling a sense of tremendous relief and gratitude. I was relieved that there was a band who were not using the first Madness album as their only reference point and I was grateful that they were speaking directly to my heart.

I loved the sunshine, the glamour, the laddish larks, the carefree wonder of Britpop but at home, alone in the night, I was plagued by darker and more troubled thoughts and I felt a sense of isolation, of worthlessness and of emotional and physical pain that couldn't be soothed by Northern Uproar. When Patrick Duff sang about nobody being able to love me in a thousand years I believed him and then when he sang that the time for the rest of my life was close by, I felt a wonderful surge of hope.

Three minute pop songs were few and far between on that first album. Strangelove were an entirely separate entity to the other bands who were making waves at this point in time. They were the sound of the morning after, the dull ache of broken hearts and the near deafening roar of the silence inside your empty room. Patrick describes them now as 'experimental' and I think that's about as good a description of what was going on as any. They were experimenting with music, with words, with sounds, with drugs and with stardom.

The results of those experiments resulted in a second album that was the best album released during the Britpop era that wasn't a Britpop record. Many people get very excited about 'OK Computer' by Radiohead and hold it up as some sort of milestone in British popular music - progressive, experimental and blah, blah, blah. Whenever I hear anyone describe that album in those sorts of terms it serves to confirm one thing for me - they haven't heard 'Love and Other Demons', because if they had then they would have realised that 'OK Computer' was nothing more than the musical equivalent of the Emperor's new clothes.

Alright.

I'm going a bit overboard with the Radiohead criticism but I'm doing it for a good reason.

You have to understand that 'Love and Other Demons' is a collection of songs that are so beautiful, so full of love, so broken, so charged and so emotionally brutal that just one listen is enough to leave you gasping for air.

I spent a lot of time before 'Love and Other Demons' was released trying to convince myself that only Morrissey understood me, but the truth is that I was trying to make myself fit the life that Morrissey was singing about. When I heard 'Love and Other Demons' I realised that the person singing actually *did* understand me, the real me. What Strangelove did was blow away the affectation and pierce the very heart of me. I listened to it over and over and over again. Each time it had the same effect. Over twenty years have passed and nothing has changed.

As I write this I'm listening to 'Beautiful Alone' and I can feel tears welling up. I'm probably just tired. It's been a long day. Or it could just be that when Smokey sings I hear violins but when Patrick sings I hear the entire string section.

One of the most striking things about Strangelove wasn't just the power of the lyrics or the charm and charisma of Patrick as a front man but the craft and guile of the musicians in the band. Alex Lee is one of the finest guitarists of his generation - a lot of attention is given to John Squire, Bernard Butler and Andy Bell when guitarists from that time are being discussed but Lee is also worthy of a place at that table. The fact that he has continued to work with a variety of other bands is testament to his ability, with Placebo, Goldfrapp, Suede and Florence and the Machine all benefiting from his talent. Julian Pransky-Poole didn't just contribute a great name, he was another fine guitarist, while Joe Allen laid down bass lines that drove the songs directly to your soul and John Langley was a genuinely brilliant drummer, crafting beats and rhythms that perfectly framed the riot of emotion that was raging in front of him.

Despite all of this though, 'Love and Other Demons' failed to make a dent in the top forty and only one of the singles, 'Beautiful Alone', made it into the singles charts. While I'm fairly sure that for Patrick, and possibly the rest of the gang, chart success was less important than simply making music, it troubled me at the time that a band I cared so much about was passing other people by. I was evangelical in my attempts to get other people to listen to them by including one of their tracks on every mix-tape I made, buying more than one copy of each of the singles (and on multiple formats too) and singing their praises whenever conversations turned to music.

I was a loyal and faithful disciple.

Twelve months later a third album arrived - 'Strangelove'.

The lead single was 'The Greatest Show on Earth' and it was as close to a Britpop record as they ever came - it could even almost qualify as a pop song. It had strings and pop culture references to Disney and Christopher Robin as well as a proper sing-along chorus. If a conscious decision had been made to be more radio friendly then it had worked as 'The Greatest Show...' made it to number 36 in the charts. It seemed, at long last, that some momentum was building behind them and that the sort of success that had catapulted lesser talents to the pop stratosphere was to be theirs for the taking.

Incredibly the next single, the towering, brutal, thumping glory that is 'Freak' failed to deliver a similar level of success and when the album appeared it too managed to avoid the top 40, charting at number 67. There was a third single, 'Another Night In', which was a brilliantly peculiar and eccentric little gem of a song, but when it too failed to set the world alight the writing was on the wall and Strangelove were over.

I've remained true to Strangelove ever since I first placed 'Time for the Rest of Your Life' onto the turntable in my desperate student accommodation in an even more desperate Scottish town in 1994. I knew from the very first listen that in Patrick Duff I had found someone I could believe in. Those songs have soundtracked some of the darkest moments and the longest nights in the years since and I've been glad of their presence. If you find yourself alone or lonely and need to hear someone who understands the awfulness of that situation then turn to Strangelove, give your heart to Patrick Duff and he will comfort you.

Chapter 18

The Baroque Pop of My Life Story

My Life Story

'Grunge was anti-fashion and rave was crap fashion.'
(Jake Shillingford, My Life Story)

Unlike lots of other bands who believe that it's the music that matters most, My Life Story are committed to the truth of pop music and popular culture - that the look is as important as anything else and indeed it may even be *more* important than anything else.

Glamour and style had been all but vanquished from the world of guitar music thanks to the dominance of Seattle bands on the world stage at the start of the 90s. Washing your hair had become an act of heresy. Wearing clothes that actually fitted your body was nothing short of blasphemy against the gods of grunge. It was a dreadful and ugly time for music and fashion.

When Shillingford unleashed the debut My Life Story single ('Girl A, Girl B, Boy C') in 1993, it was a statement of intent. It was an orchestral manoeuvre from the dark edges of forgotten British pop glories. It was obvious even at that stage that My Life Story were not bandwagon jumpers, but were instead a band who had arrived with a clear vision and manifesto for what pop music could and should be.

Their grandiose, orchestral, baroque sound was forged in the soul of Jake Shillingford as far back as 1973.

JS *'Block Buster!' by The Sweet was the first record bought for me by my parents and the first record I bought was 'Oliver's Army' by Elvis Costello and the Attractions. It felt, to me at least, that certain elements within glam, punk and then new wave were relentlessly creating original ideas and performance styles. Then I fell in love with the 1980s Liverpool scene where bands like The Pale Fountains, Echo and the Bunnymen, Wah and Julian Cope too were all using guitars and strings.'*

Mark Morriss of The Bluetones describes his band as 'frilly shirts surrounded by Fred Perry'. Lots of people forget that, in reality, Britpop wasn't really ever a genre, it was a description of a wider popular cultural uprising.

JS *'I always thought Fred Perrys were a bit of an obvious modernist revivalist statement. I quickly found my own tailor! We were around the scene very early on, which was very much London based. Britpop as we know it came out of north and central London and the initial crop of bands were reacting to the lack of stage presence and glamour that the American grunge and British rave scenes were supplying.*

I was part of a group of people that would debate in pubs about the death of the pop star. In some ways our debut single in 1993, 'Girl A, Girl B, Boy C' was about anonymity and isolation. Certainly in London there was a movement towards fashion and music combining together for the first time in a long time.

Grunge was anti fashion and rave was crap fashion. A baggy white jumpsuit was part of the drug scene and we were reacting against that.

We were always conveniently either 'in' Britpop or 'out' of it.

Britpop as a term has never restricted us, it has only opened doors. I am proud to be British and I am proud that I write pop music.'

'Mornington Crescent' is one of the best albums released during the Britpop era, in many ways it nods to the 60s, while its rejection of the ordinary, its embracing of glamour and its London-ness make it *the* Britpop album.

JS *'I had recently met Anthony Newley, whose singing style I had always admired. Newley was the biggest influence on David Bowie and it seemed to me only natural to go right back to the source where great theatrical pop music comes from.*

In addition to that, both Julian Cope and Marc Almond had released compilation albums of Scott Walker songs, which were never off my turntable. But my great obsession is John Barry. His arrangement and attention to detail in his orchestrations has no comparison.'

That just about sums up the allure of My Life Story - grandiose, urban and full of love. Those are things that once made Morrissey an idol to the outsiders.

JS *'I actually met Morrissey in 1995 when he came to see the band at the Water Rats in Kings Cross, and then at the Jazz Café some weeks later.*

He was working with Steve Lilywhite on the album 'Southpaw Grammar' and Steve at that time was interested in producing what would have become 'The Golden Mile', but we didn't have a record deal.'

When music hall legend Billy Merson recorded William Hargreaves' song 'The Night I Appeared as Macbeth' in the early 1920s, it was, in very many ways, the earliest example of what would become, nearly seventy years later, Britpop. With more than a hint of nostalgia and a romantic vision of London life, the song is also witty and, at times, laugh out loud funny. You can hear echoes of people like Merson, in flashes, on records by Blur (most obviously) but also in things like Thurman's 'English Tea' or The Weekenders' 'All Grown Up' and, much more obviously, in the work of David Devant and His Spirit Wife. There is one line in the song that always makes me chuckle: *'They made me a present of Mornington Crescent, they threw it one brick at a time'*.

Ah, Mornington Crescent.

Home to Spencer Gore, first president of the Camden Town Group, a gathering of English Post-Impressionist painters who would meet at the home of Walter Sickert, who also lived on the street for a time. Gore painted several views from his home at 31 Mornington Crescent.

Sickert, for his part, was living at 6 Mornington Crescent when the Camden Town Murder took place in 1907 and he later renamed a series of his paintings, which featured a clothed man and a nude woman on a bed, to reflect his interest in the case.

It is the work of another artist that is most closely associated with the Crescent in the minds, and hearts, of a certain type of forty-something individual though. A quarter of a century ago, Jake Shillingford gathered a gaggle of musicians to breathe life into the grand baroque pop, orchestral manoeuvres and sixties soaked songs that were buzzing around his heart and soul. The result of that was an album that, possibly more than any other of the period, captures the spirit of nineties London, a time when Cool Britannia seemed, however unlikely this sounds now, to be something more than just a marketing soundbite, a time when anything and everything seemed possible and a time when we all wanted to sparkle.

'Mornington Crescent' was released to absolutely no fanfare.

It reached number 115 in the charts.

Two of the three singles released from the album didn't chart and the third, a song called 'You Don't Sparkle (In My Eyes)' reached the high spot of number 155 in the singles charts.

It wasn't that nobody was listening - I was and I played my part in propelling 'Sparkle' to the bottom of the hit parade. People were listening, it's just that there was not enough of us. 'Mornington Crescent' is a staggering, swaggering, shimmering, slinky and, whisper it, sexy album filled to bursting with Bond themes for Bond films that never were and the sort of sixties pop that bands in the sixties couldn't have dared dream of producing. It was the musical equivalent of a pair of tailor made trousers from Chittleborough & Morgan: mohair, frog mouth pockets, cut on the ankle, no belt loops, fully lined. Proper.

The problem for 'Mornington Crescent' lay not in the fact that it wasn't any good but in the fact that by January 1995 Britpop was associated by the general public with trainers, tracksuit tops, beer, Oasis and Loaded. The thrilling and frilly shirted delights of a baroque pop group were always going to find it difficult to break through. They did though, eventually, and that meant people could discover the album at last and help to cement its reputation as one of the greatest albums of the era.

You can have the stifled yawn of 'Wonderwall' if you want it.

Me?

I'll take '(Theme From) Checkmate'.

You can have the sonic flaccid member of 'Country House' if you want it.

Me?

I'll take the glittery stomp of 'Motorcade'.

You can have the familiar (but still wonderful) 'Common People' if you want it.

Me?

I'll take the aching swoop and soar of 'You Don't Sparkle (In My Eyes)'.

This was the sound of youth, of a generation finding the confidence to suggest that maybe, just maybe, we could be *better* than we had been. That we could cast an eye to the past for inspiration but then craft something defiantly modern from that. This was the sound of the hope that was going to blow a despised government out of office and usher in the prospect of something better. This was the sound of style meeting substance. This was the sound of Saturday night at the local dance palace but stripped of the malice that usually soaks the crowd at closing time. This was the sound of first love revisited in every love. This was the soundtrack to our lives - or at least to the lives we wanted to live. The second album, 'Golden Mile' is another glorious gem. It broke into the top 40 at a time when you had to physically sell records to achieve that. For a band making the sort of music that My Life Story were making and looking the way they did, flamboyant, eccentric and camp, that was a massive achievement.

JS '*I always felt at the time that MLS and our incredible fans lived in a self-imposed bubble where we always knew that we were different from anything else that was going on. We shared a sensibility that as Britpop became more mainstream, MLS and our fans seemed to feel more of a clique. But that has always suited me. I always wanted to offer something different.*'

Chapter 19

Wha's Like Us?

Scotland.

A land of stunning natural beauty.

A land that has helped shape the modern world thanks to the enlightenment and its contribution to science and medicine.

A land of outstanding artistic, literary and musical heritage.

In the interests of fairness it's also worth pointing out that it is a land where the people have decided that the best means of attack in a street fight is to use your own face as a weapon and where the Bay City Rollers still sell out venues that bands who actually care about music would struggle to half fill. Oh, we also deep fry everything. That's not a stereotype, it's an absolute statement of fact.

From this greedy and fairly pleasant land have come more top ranking bands than seems fair. For every lump of hideousness like the aforementioned Bay City Rollers there are three or four bands that could bend your mind, melt your heart and lift your spirits: Orange Juice, Josef K, The Pastels, Bis, Aztec Camera, Love and Money, Hipsway, Belle and Sebastian, Primal Scream, BMX Bandits - all incredible bands with more wonderful songs between them than the entire 'Now...' back catalogue could muster between now and the end of the world.

During the Britpop years there were a handful of hardy Scottish souls who could be tossed into the salad of Britpop - The Gyres, Whiteout, Geneva, Bis and Travis (for at least one album) were all part of the scene. One other band also appeared at this point and contributed one of the toppermost and poppermost albums of the entire era, The Supernaturals.

Lead singer and guitarist James McColl had been influenced by all the right sorts of bands before forming The Supernaturals in 1991.

JM '*For me it was those 60s and 70s bands like The Monkees, The Move, Slade, Madness, Blondie and The Police. As far as the band was concerned though it was bands like The Cardigans, Teenage Fanclub, The Replacements, Fountains of Wayne, You Am I and a LOT of the Britpop bands: Dodgy, Boo Radleys, Blur, Oasis and so on. At that time those bands would put out records and everyone would buy them, share them and we'd take bits of them!*'

After a few years of touring relentlessly and releasing two mini-albums on cassette ('Big 7' and 'Dark Star' were both released in 1993) the band eventually came to the attention of Andy Ross at Food Records and were signed in 1995.

JM '*We were touring around the Highlands of Scotland doing our own thing, writing songs and then, in the early 90s the British music scene came 'round to our sound, which was very lucky for us in retrospect.*'

They spent the bulk of the following year writing, recording and touring. It wasn't just the fact that they were touring but who they were touring with that catches the eye. The list of bands they supported reads like a fantasy Britpop festival line-up - Ash, The Bluetones, Menswe@r, Sleeper and Dodgy.

JM '*Martin Rossiter (Gene) saw us playing keepie uppies during a soundcheck and came down with a pair of Cuban heeled boots and a 3 piece suit on and did ball tricks worthy of a Premiership* *footballer. Gene were really decent guys as were all of those bands. We had bought most of their records like 'Giant Steps', the Dodgy album and the first couple of Bluetones singles. Me and Derek had been to see Dodgy at King Tuts along with about eight other people on their first tour. We were fans basically. You'd finish your set then enjoy watching bands you liked. Pretty good really looking back! Took it for granted at the time.'*

'Smile' was the first single released from their, as yet, unreleased debut album and despite the fact that it failed to chart (at least in 1996) it served as a fabulous snapshot of the band. The influence of The Monkees and Madness are obvious - it's a wonderfully upbeat, jolly melody undercut by some deliciously off message lyrics.

The next single was 'Lazy Lover' and this time the public were paying a bit more attention and it broke the top forty, peaking at number thirty four. It's a genuinely funny piece of pop magnificence. A tale of a relationship beyond repair as the male of the species just can't get the energy up to get into bed with his 'delicious' partner because he'd rather be doing something else instead. Like Half Man Half Biscuit, McColl had the ability to write things that were funny without ever slipping into novelty record territory.

'It Doesn't Matter Anymore' arrived in 1997 and delivered on the promise of those two singles. Twelve bona fide, solid gold, authentic, genuine pop songs that had your fingers snappin' and your heart jumping into your mouth. From the sublime 'I Don't Think So' to the ridiculously brilliant 'Stammer' this was an album that dared you to lift the needle, hit skip or fast forward, but you couldn't because every song was the equal of the one before it and the one after too. It's an album that plays like a greatest hits collection. Two more singles (and the re-issued 'Smile') saw the album thrust its way into the top ten. They were pop stars.

On the opposite side of the Britpop coin were another Scottish band who had more in common with the post-punk world of Joy Division, Echo and the Bunnymen and The Smiths than The Monkees or The Beatles.

They were Geneva.

It was a beautiful day.

The sun was shining.

Shirt sleeves.

T-shirts.

Summer dresses.

For the more daring boys - shorts.

Well, to *me* that was daring.

I wouldn't dare.

This is the summer of 1997 and this is the V festival in Leeds.

I had turned twenty-four a month earlier, I had finished with university and I had a job.

I was in a relationship.

A real one.

I was, in fact, engaged.

We don't need to dwell.

We had driven to Leeds in my Vauxhall Combo van - all those years studying sociology and politics, striving for a Diploma in Social Work, and I was delivering fizzy brown water in a white van. Time well spent I think we can all agree.

Sometimes we would sleep in the back of that van.

I hadn't ever gone to a festival before.

I didn't like the idea.

I was here because Gene were playing, as well as The Bluetones, The Longpigs and Echobelly.

I had watched Stereophonics, The Supernaturals and Hurricane #1 and then gone for a walk during Veruca Salt

I had no room in my life, or in my heart, for Veruca Salt, mainly because they were a bit too grunge friendly. I think that was probably a mistake. I've grown to accept them, even like them in the years since. The culture wars of the nineties were no place for half-heartedness, you were either on one side or the other. It was a bit like Brexit. But more unpleasant.

Then Geneva took the stage.

I have no idea what the first song was.

I have no idea what any of the songs were.

I know that they played almost all of the songs I would come to love in the weeks and months after this but, right then, I didn't know anything.

That's not true.

I did know *something*.

The moment Andrew Montgomery opened his mouth I felt sure that there was something sublime in the world. Something beautiful. Something better. Something better than me. Something worth my time. Something that could help me. Something that could make things better.

He sang.

People listened.

I heard.

I heard the truth of how he was singing.

It wouldn't have mattered what he was singing.

Pure.

Clean.

Untouched.

Heavenly.

You need to understand something here - I wasn't a real person in 1997. It is possible that I have never been a real person. I was sad and a little bit broken on the inside then. I am sad and a little bit broken on the inside now. There was no reason for that. There is no reason for that but it is still true.

I have just come back from the cinema where, in the dark, I cried from the moment the lights went down - not constantly but infrequently, yet regularly, throughout the film. Sad little tears filling sadder little eyes then wending their way down my sad little cheeks.

For no reason.

It was the same when Andrew Montgomery started singing on that sunny afternoon.

Tears welling in my eyes.

Tears born of relief.

Amongst all the ugliness of my own emotions, I had something beautiful to cling to.

Other people heard him sing 'Tranquilizer' from the stage in Leeds, but I heard a prayer. No, that's not accurate; I felt a prayer forming inside my heart. Pleading to a God that I was beginning to doubt wanted me to be happy - whatever happiness was. Whatever happiness is. I don't know.

I do know.

I've experienced it.

I've felt it.

Sunlight bathed the golden glow.

That was probably the moment when I fell for Geneva.

One line.

Heard in a field in Leeds.

Twenty-two years ago.

I heard it again just a few months ago when Andrew Montgomery took the stage at Star Shaped in Glasgow. I felt the same things as I had back then. I could even feel the sun of that summer's day despite being in the beginnings of a miserable Scottish winter. I heard that line again and then I felt those things again.

Heard the voice.

Felt the prayer form.

'Cast me adrift on a dream.'

We're not in Leeds anymore, Toto.

I am in my bedsit in Johnstone.

A bedroom with stacks of NME and Melody Maker littering the floor.

On the walls, centrefolds from Loaded because I thought that was what it meant to be a man.

New lad.

All surface.

No feeling.

Then the album, 'Further', descended from some celestial realm and it was all feeling.

That was what I wanted.

A yearning to be somewhere, anywhere, else.

A burning desire to be someone, anyone, else.

I wanted a dream.

Not the dream that I was having.

An awful repetitive, recurring nightmare where a single shiny pin was in my mouth and each time I tried to remove it, it multiplied, over and over again, until my mouth was filled with pins.

Take it away, Mr Freud.

Not just songs.

Music.

Emotions.

Feelings.

Hymns for the living dead.

It's easy to judge.

Easier still to laugh.

It takes character to be gentle and kind.

For some life really is, at least every so often, too much.

We don't need to cheer up.

We don't need to pick ourselves up.

Who knows what we need.

Broken souls.

Unfinished.

Wings that are temporary - we can take flight but the crash is inevitable.

It is difficult to describe the impact of songs like 'No One Speaks' or 'Into the Blue' on someone like me.

'Have you ever had suicidal thoughts?' the doctor asked me the other day as I sat weeping in her room trying to explain where I was.

'No. But sometimes I would like to disappear.'

Then 'Into the Blue' started playing in my head.

Or in my heart.

There is a moment on 'Further' when Andrew Montgomery describes the way in which someone he once loved has changed, becoming something that he no longer needs or desires, something that he can live without.

That is the greatest fear.

That people will see you for who you really are, warts and all.

They will watch as you reveal the truth and then they will realise that they could do without.

Agony.

These are universal feelings.

These are ever present emotions.

The grotesque of the everyday.

The loneliness that lies around the corner.

Geneva captured all of that.

Geneva captured all of this.

Then they gave it back to us.

Let us feel it.

Suddenly we could feel something else.

Hope.

We are not alone.

Other people...

Other people...

Like you...

Like me...

People.

Hope for the hopeless.

A prayer answered.

Faith, in something, restored.

From a field in Leeds to a room in Johnstone.

From that relationship to the real thing.

Beauty in poetry.

Poetry from pain.

Heart and soul.

This is all very far away from the popular image of nineties Britain, of Cool Britannia and Britpop. There is no cocaine soaked swagger here, no one is mad for it and there are no middle-class, working class affectations. And while the joy of the era may well have sat at the feet of 'Parklife' era Blur and the biggest impact may have been caused by Oasis, the real power and heart of the era was found in bands like Geneva.

Greenock sits on the West coast of Scotland and on the surface is a fairly genteel sort of a town. It's a bit more upmarket than its neighbour Port Glasgow, but it is still, like so many towns in that part of Scotland, marked by decades of industrial decline and under-investment.

Which makes it fertile soil for dreamers and schemers.

Back in the early part of the nineties, a gaggle of too cool for school boys found themselves with dreams of being rock 'n' roll stars. Inspired, like so many others, by the second summer of love and, specifically, by the sounds of The Stone Roses they turned their attentions to Manchester, England and to America's West Coast for inspiration.

They became Whiteout and followed in the footsteps of the Roses by becoming the first band to sign to the Silvertone label following their success.

Soon enough they found themselves with a dedicated local following and then found themselves heading out on tour with a similarly inspired gaggle of rough boys from Manchester called Oasis. History may have led some people to believe that Oasis stole the show on that tour but the truth, as ever, is less pure and less simple than that. The Whiteout boys were more than capable of holding their own and they won hearts and minds along the way.

In 1994, they released their debut single 'No Time' and found themselves playing it live on The Word. You can go and check out that footage and then come back and tell me that it doesn't set your pulse racing. Everything about it is perfect - attitude, wardrobe, hair and melodies. Like all genuinely great bands, Whiteout looked like a gang. The sort of gang you wished you could be a part of but, if you are anything like me, you knew you never could be.

Cool is cool.

It should have been the start of something.

It should have been a brilliant career.

Instead, it fizzed too briefly then faded away.

The best band to come out of Greenock ever?

Definitely. No, maybe.

The best Scottish band of the nineties?

Tricky when the competition includes some big names, but I reckon they deserve to be considered and perhaps even crowned.

They had it all.

Just listen to 'Detroit' or 'Thirty-eight' or 'Shine On You' or 'Altogether' from their incredible debut album 'Bite It' and tell me that Bolan and Visconti wouldn't have cut their fingers off for any of them.

Epilogue

There will be people who, having read this book, will be angry about the omission of certain bands. They will be unhappy that there is no coverage of Cast, Ocean Colour Scene, Shed Seven, Northern Uproar or even Menswe@r. I understand that anger and unhappiness. I have felt it when I have read other books about Britpop that have focused, almost exclusively, on those same bands while pointedly ignoring some of the bands that I have focused on instead.

The truth is that it isn't really possible to write a book about Britpop that would make everyone who claims to love the era happy, because everybody has their own version of the story. For some people Oasis and Paul Weller are the giants of the scene while for me, they had nothing to do with it. When I was sitting on the overnight bus from Glasgow Buchanan Street to London's Victoria coach station I wasn't listening to 'Wonderwall' or 'Peacock Suit', I wasn't getting ready for a night on the dance-floor soundtracked by 'Alright' and I didn't have a Stone Island parka or a bucket hat in my overnight bag. That wasn't my Britpop experience.

I wasn't a lad, a dad or a trad rocker. I was a pop kid, a fop and, in my mind, a dandy. My soundtrack was Pimlico and David Devant, Whiteout and Tiny Monroe, Elcka and Strangelove, Pulp and Suede, Blur and Mantaray, Denim and The Auteurs. My crowd were the uncommon people of 'Common People'.

I couldn't have written something that wasn't honest about my experience on the frontline of a pop culture revolution. I had to write about what it was really all about and what it was really like for a kid like me, living in a coastal town in Scotland where ambition burned low and where dressing a bit like Jarvis Cocker at any point before 1995 would have resulted in physical violence from the boys who would later form the core demographic for the likes of Oasis.

When I first started writing about Britpop in 2017 I was motivated by a desire to remind myself of a moment in time when everything had seemed possible and within reach. It wasn't just about the music, it was about the life that the music helped to create.

Then I started to write stuff for people to read, which meant that, at times, I was writing what I thought people wanted to hear. That isn't a good place to be, it is a form of click-bait. This book is my attempt to return to something more honest. That's why it isn't *the* story of Britpop or the definitive story of Cool Britannia. It's just *a* story of a point in time.

I know that for every person who is cross about my take on Oasis or my refusal to write about some other band they love, there will be many more people who are delighted to see a version of the story that more closely resembles their own. I wrote this for you.

About the Author

Paul Laird is a teacher and writer based in Edinburgh. Since 2015 he has run the Mild Mannered Army, a pop culture website which has a particular focus on the Britpop era. He also hosts the Mild Mannered Army podcast where he has interviewed several important figures from that period including Stephen Street (producer of several key Britpop albums including Blur's 'Life trilogy), James and Jude Cook (authors and former members of Flamingoes), Rick McMurray (Ash), Matt James (Gene), Mikey B. Georgeson (David Devant and His Spirit Wife), Daniel Rachel (author of 'Don't Look Back in Anger'), Matt Glasby (author of 'Britpop Cinema'), Jake Shillingford (My Life Story) and many other musicians and writers. He has been a contributor to BBC Radio Scotland's 'Classic Scottish Albums' series where he has discussed the cultural impact of albums from The Bluebells, Idlewild, K.T Tunstall, Hipsway and The Delgados.